Grades 5-6

Reader's Theater...

and So Much More!

Grades 5-6

Reader's Theater...

and So Much More!

Brenda McGee and Debbie Keiser

Cover Art and Illustrations by Brandon Bolt

Prufrock Press Inc.
Waco, Texas

Edited by Sarah Morrison

Production Design by Raquel Trevino

ISBN-13: 978-1-59363-501-5

Prufrock Press Inc.
P.O. Box 8813
Waco, TX 76714-8813
Phone: (800) 998-2208
Fax: (800) 240-0333
http://www.prufrock.com

TABLE OF CONTENTS

TO THE TEACHER

Overview

Reader's Theater is a thinking, reading, writing, speaking, and listening experience. Readers should rely on their vocal abilities to portray a character. Students should strive for voice flexibility, crisp articulation, proper pronunciation, and projection.

These plays and skits are not meant to be staged performances. There is no need for sets, elaborate props, or costumes. However, it might be fun to add more drama to the Reader's Theaters with minimal stage direction and easy-to-find props.

If you decide you would like to make one or more of the Reader's Theaters into major productions, it is suggested that students work in committees and divide up the responsibilities for creating a live performance. This could involve everything from designing scenery to writing invitations and programs. The experience could also provide an economics lesson in using budgets and selling concessions.

These Reader's Theaters were written for all students to enjoy as they develop their senses of humor; improve their oral communication skills; increase their knowledge of content; gain fluency, comprehension, and self-confidence; and boost their interest in reading.

The Reader's Theater Language Arts Skills listed on the next page will be practiced during the performance of all of the Reader's Theaters. Students will also have opportunities to use writing, research, and other skills as they complete pre, post, and extension activities found in each play.

Management

Scan the plays and assign parts you believe would fit a student's comfort level based on his or her reading ability.

Give students an opportunity to read their parts silently and ask questions about any unfamiliar words. The objective is fluency and oral expression, not cold reading.

If there are too many characters, assign students with smaller parts more than one character. If you have too few parts, cut some of the longer parts into more than one part. Another option is to challenge students, as a class or in small groups, to create more characters and add more parts.

Even the most reluctant and shy students enjoy Reader's Theaters. This is "learning can be fun" at its best!

Reader's Theater Language Arts Skills

Sight-Word Reading
✦ Reads numerous high-frequency words fluently

Vocabulary Development
✦ Learns new vocabulary by listening, reading, or receiving instruction

Comprehending What Is Read
✦ Uses context clues to determine words' meanings
✦ Predicts and verifies outcomes
✦ Recognizes and analyzes characters, setting, and plot in a passage listened to or read
✦ Makes and explains inferences and supports them with evidence from text
✦ Identifies facts and details
✦ Identifies the main idea (explicit and implicit) of a passage
✦ Draws conclusions and supports them with evidence from the text

Literary Response
✦ Retells a story without using the book, including beginning, middle, and end
✦ When retelling a story, includes important events and details
✦ Summarizes or paraphrases text
✦ Identifies the correct sequence of events in a story through retelling or acting out

Oral Communication
✦ Speaks to an audience using appropriate volume and rate
✦ Adapts oral language to purpose, audience, and occasion

♦ Presents dramatic interpretations
♦ Presents to an audience

Listening Skills
♦ Listens actively and purposefully
♦ Listens to, enjoys, and appreciates spoken language

Humor Terms in Literature

Exaggeration—to make something greater than it actually is; to stretch or magnify the truth

Farce—an exaggerated comedy based on broadly humorous situations; a play intended only to be funny; an absurd or ridiculous situation

Figure of speech—any phrase or saying that is not meant to be taken literally, including idioms, hyperbole, and the like

Hyperbole—an exaggeration in writing used to make a point

Idiom—a phrase that has a particular meaning other than its literal (word-for-word) meaning

Irony—when the audience expects a certain thing to happen, but then the opposite happens

Metaphor—a literary device in which two unlike things are compared without using "like" or "as"

Onomatopoeia—words that sound like the noises they describe, such as "swish," "woof," and "splat"

Oxymoron—a literary device in which two contradictory words are used together to describe something

Parody—a literary or artistic work that imitates the characteristic style of an author; a work for comic effect or ridicule

Pun—the humorous use of a word or words that are formed similarly or sound alike, but that have different meanings, made in order to play on two or more of the possible applications; a play on words

Sarcasm—a taunting, sneering, cutting, or caustic remark; a gibe or jeer, generally ironic

Satire—a manner of writing that mixes a critical attitude with wit and humor in an effort to improve humankind and human institutions

Simile—a literary device in which a comparison is made between two things using either "like" or "as"

Understatement—expressing an idea with less emphasis or in a lesser degree than is called for; the opposite of hyperbole; mostly used for ironic emphasis

Notes

_____

_____

_____

_____

_____

_____

_____

_____

_____

_____

_____

_____

_____

Act 1
READER'S THEATERS

IN THE BEGINNING THERE WAS THE WHEEL

Pre-Reading Suggestions:

Assessing Prior Knowledge
✦ Create a Known-Want to Learn-Learned (K-W-L) chart. Draw a simple outline of an automobile and divide it into three sections. Use the first section to assess what students already know about the history of the automobile industry. Use the other two sections to record what students want to know and what they learned.

Making Predictions
✦ Tell students that the play they will read is a brief history of the automobile industry. Ask students to discuss the following: If they had written this play, where would they have started, and how would they have told the story?

Identifying Facts and Details
✦ Explain that this play is written in seven acts. Each act covers a particular span of time. Challenge students to record facts or details that don't really fit the time period. Have students hold their notes for discussion until the end of the play.

Post-Reading Suggestions:

Acts 1–4

Making Predictions
✦ Ask students to share the predictions they made before the play began. Where did this play begin, and how did the author tell the story of the automobile industry?

Identifying Facts and Details
✦ Have students begin filling in the last section of the car outline, "What I Learned." Ask students if they heard anything in Act 1 that did not seem

to fit with the time period (e.g., cave people talking in well-developed language, reference to marriage).

- ✧ What about Act 2? (There were no travel games to buy then.)
- ✧ What about Act 3? (The words "automobile" and "American Dream" weren't used then.)
- ✧ What about Act 4? (People probably didn't "high-five" back then.)

Expressing Ideas in Writing

◆ In Act 4, Frank Duryea says that having his car break down during the first public test was the most embarrassing moment in his life. Have students write a paragraph describing their most embarrassing moment. Assure students they will not have to share unless they wish.

Retelling a Story Including Important Events and Details

◆ Have students form four groups. Assign each group one of the four acts of the play. Have each group reread the act, then organize and plan how it will retell that part of the story to the rest of the class.

Acts 5–7

Identifying Facts and Details

◆ Complete the middle section of the car outline, "What I Would Like to Know."

Independent Reading and Research

◆ Fill in the final section of the car, "What I Learned." Leave this section up in a corner of the room. Furnish reference books that may help students discover the answers to any questions they have. This can be an ongoing project. Be sure to have students share their discoveries at some point.

Expressing Ideas in Writing

◆ Have students work in groups of three or four to discuss what might happen in Act 8. Have them write a brief outline or summary that they will share with the class. After all ideas have been shared and discussed, have students go back to their groups and write Act 8.

Sequential Order

◆ Have students form three groups. Have each group illustrate six to eight major events that happened during the development of the automobile. Place the drawings in sequential order and display them.

IN THE BEGINNING THERE WAS THE WHEEL
ACT I

Cast of Characters
Narrator
Cave Person 1
Cave Person 2
Cave Person 3

Setting
Outside, near caves and hills

Optional Props
Items to carry on back that look heavy

Narrator: (*standing to the left of the stage*) In the beginning, humans lived in caves with their families and a few close friends and relatives. There wasn't much need for automobiles, because there really wasn't any place to go. There was, however, a need for the wheel. The time is 12,000 B.C.

Cave Person 1: (*carrying what seems like a heavy burden*) I can't believe that I, Grog, have to carry heavy burdens over hills to my wife, Grogina, and little Grogletts.

Cave Person 2: (*carrying a heavy burden also*) I hear that! Must be an easier way to get things from one place to other.

Cave Person 3: (*carrying a heavy burden*) How about cart with wheels?

Cave Person 1: (*stops to look at Cave Person 3*) What's that?

Cave Person 3: (*stops, scratches head, looks very puzzled*) I don't know where that came from. (*shrugs shoulders*) Just forget I said that!

Cave Person 1: (*speaking to Cave Person 2*) He's losing it! Must be the heat!

Cave Person 2: (*grunts in agreement*)

Cave People: (*walk off stage, continuing to carry heavy burdens*)

Narrator: Eventually the wheel was developed, and it greatly improved people's ability to move things from one place to another. That was the beginning of humankind's need for transportation and the automobile.

ACT II

Note to Teacher

✦ Make three large signs that read "100 Years." You may opt to have students create the signs before the play begins.

Cast of Characters	**Setting**
Narrator	Riding in a covered wagon on the
3 Sign Carriers	plains
Pioneer Man	
Pioneer Woman	**Props**
2 Pioneer Children	3 signs that say "100 Years"
	2 chairs

Narrator: Hundreds of years went by. (***three students with signs that say "100 Years" walk across the stage***) People started harnessing animals to wheels, because that made moving objects and people much easier. Hundreds of years went by. (***same three students with signs walk across the stage***) People discovered other people in different parts of the world, so they decided to visit. Some even moved their entire families. Carriages were invented (***sign carriers walk by***), then stagecoaches (***sign carriers walk by***), then covered wagons. The need for the automobile was getting greater and greater. The time is now 1750. I told you hundreds of years went by!

(*two pioneers sit in chairs at the front of the "covered wagon"; two pioneer children sit on the floor behind them*)

Pioneer Man: (*holding imaginary reins to the horses*) Things sure are going to be different when we get to Texas. No more busy streets like ours where sometimes as many as three carriages pass by our house within an hour.

Pioneer Woman: (*sitting next to Pioneer Man*) Yes-sir-ee! We'll have a piece of land that nobody else has ever seen. Nobody will drop by for days, weeks, or even months.

Pioneer Children: (*tap pioneer parents on the shoulders and take turns saying lines*)

> Are we there yet?
> I'm hungry!
> I'm bored!
> I want to go back home.
> Didn't you buy any travel games for us to play?

Pioneer Man: (*turning around and acting frustrated*) Now, settle down back there! We've got miles to go yet. Don't make me come back there! If you two don't sit still, I'm gonna turn this wagon around . . .

Narrator: Some say that this was the start of the American family vacation.

ACT III

Cast of Characters	**Setting**
Narrator 1	Inside a steam car on a busy street
Narrator 2	
Captain Nicholas Joseph Cugnot	**Props**
Private Knothead	2 chairs
Steam Car Driver (man)	1 red scarf or flag
Steam Car Passenger (woman)	
Freddie (signal person)	

Narrator 1: The first road vehicle that could travel by itself was a steam car. Just imagine a great big teakettle with three wheels. It was invented in 1769 by French army captain Joseph Cugnot.

Narrator 2: It hauled cannons, traveled just 3 miles per hour, and had to stop every 10 or 15 minutes to build up steam.

Captain Cugnot: (*speaks with a French accent, is seated in a chair with Private Knothead pretending to walk beside him*) What do you think of my invention now, Private Knothead? (*car stops to build up steam, Private Knothead stops pretending to walk*)

Private Knothead: (*speaks with a French accent*) It is great, sir! At this rate, we might actually get to the battle before everyone goes home. (*starts pretending to walk*)

Captain Cugnot: (*slightly annoyed at the private's comment*) Say what you will, but I plan to get rich off this invention, and I want to be alive to spend my money! People are going to become very dependent on the automobile. You mark my words!

Narrator 1: Steam-powered vehicles that could carry passengers were developed in England around 1801. Unfortunately, steam carriages annoyed many people. These early cars were noisy, frightened horses, dirtied the air with smoke, and scattered hot coals. Sometimes the coals set fire to crops or wooden bridges.

Narrator 2: A law was passed in 1865 that limited the speed of steam vehicles to 4 miles per hour on country roads and 2 miles per hour in cities. The law also required a signalman to walk ahead of each steam carriage to warn of its approach. The signalman carried a red flag during the day and a red lantern at night.

Steam Car Driver: (*sitting in a chair next to passenger, bouncing up and down slowly, holding the steering wheel with one hand and the brake handle with the other; the signal person walks in front, waving a red scarf or flag and stomping out hot coals*) Dear, since we can only drive 2 miles an hour now, don't you think it would be just as easy to walk to church on Sundays? After all, we only live two blocks away, and we have to wake Freddie up to be our signalman on his one day off. Freddie, get that hot coal that just flew onto the dentist's porch! (*Freddie runs to stomp it out and then gets back to the front of the car*)

Steam Car Passenger: (*looking snobbish*) Absolutely not! I wouldn't dream of letting Gertrude see me walk when we have a perfectly beautiful Stanley Steamer parked in our barn. Don't be ridiculous! We depend on our car for more than just getting from one place to another or carrying heavy loads. Cars send people a message. Our car says, "Look at how well we are doing!" That's an important part of the American Dream, you know. Stop being so practical!

Steam Car Driver: (*pointing frantically*) Freddie, there goes another one! Get it, quick! I can't afford to rebuild the school again!

Freddie: (*yawning from lack of sleep, waving a red scarf or flag, stomping out flying hot coals*) Steam car, coming through! Steam car, coming through!

Narrator 1: Steam cars didn't last past the early 1900s.

Narrator 2: Besides the obvious drawbacks, many people were just plain scared to drive a vehicle that depended on an open fire and hot steam!

ACT IV

Cast of Characters
Narrator 1
Narrator 2
Charles Duryea (dure-yay)
Frank Duryea

Setting
Sitting inside a car factory

Narrator 1: The electric car gained some popularity during the late 1890s and early 1900s. Electric cars were easy to operate, ran quietly, and did not give off smelly fumes or dangerous sparks.

Narrator 2: On the downside, however, few went faster than 20 miles per hour, and their batteries had to be recharged about every 50 miles. The electric car was a great improvement over the steam car, but it quickly lost its popularity and the interest of investors with the invention of the gasoline-powered car.

Narrator 1: Most experts agree that the Duryea brothers, Charles and Frank, built the first successful American gasoline-powered automobile.

Narrator 2: They also established the first American company to manufacture gasoline-powered automobiles.

Charles Duryea: (*clapping brother on shoulder and shaking hands*) Well, brother, congratulations on a job well done. We'll be sittin' pretty now. We'll make a future.

Frank Duryea: (*shaking hands and looking happy*) Congratulations to you too, brother. I was a little worried there for a while when our car broke down during its first public test. It was one of my most embarrassing moments. But I guess you're right. We can kick back and just wait for the money to roll in.

Charles: (*looking concerned*) Then you aren't worried about those three guys we heard about the other day?

Frank: (*looking puzzled*) Who are you talking about?

Charles: A man by the name of Henry Ford, another man named Henry Leland, and a third man named Ransom Eli Olds.

Frank: Are you kidding? We're famous. It wasn't Ford, Leland, or Olds who won the "Race of the Century." It was us, in our two-cylinder Duryea Motor Wagon. We are celebrities. We started our own company and have built 13 cars this year.

Charles: That's right, and don't forget, one of our cars is being used in the Barnum & Bailey Circus. We are kings of the automobile industry! (*high-fives his brother*)

ACT V

Cast of Characters	**Props**
Narrator 1	2 chairs
Narrator 2	
English Mechanic	
Henry Ford	
William Durant	

Narrator 1: The Duryea brothers did make a valuable contribution to the automobile industry, but that was all. Because of envy and greed, their partnership and friendship ended soon after they won the race.

Narrator 2: By 1900, more than 100 brands of cars—or horseless carriages, as they were called then—were being built and sold in the United States. Because early cars had to be handmade, they were very expensive. Most people hated to see horseless carriages come their way. The cars scared horses, turned over vegetable carts, hit people, and were resented by poor and middle-class people who couldn't afford them. In spite of the problems, the car gained popularity.

Narrator 1: The Duryea brothers should have worried more about Olds, Leland, and Ford. Ransom Eli Olds, founder of the Olds Motor Works in Detroit, built 425 gasoline-powered automobiles in 1901. This was the beginning of mass production and the assembly line.

Narrator 2: Interchangeable parts for cars were developed by Henry M. Leland, president of the Cadillac Automobile Company. This means that you could put a part from one car into any other car of the same model. To prove his point, Leland sent jumbled parts of three Cadillacs in a large box to some mechanics in England.

English Mechanic: (*speaking with an English accent*) When I opened that box, I thought the bloke had gone daft, goofy in the head. No way could me friends, the best automobile technicians in all of Europe, put this mess together into three complete cars. But we did, by George! Right snappy-looking vehicles, too, if I do say so myself.

Narrator 1: Henry Ford improved the assembly line method, invented the moving assembly line, and figured out ways to cut the cost of making a car.

Narrator 2: In 1908, Ford reached his goal. The Ford Model T took little more than an hour-and-a-half to build and sold for around $850.

Henry Ford: (*seated in what could be a car*) Yes, my cars were the most popular cars in America for nearly 20 years. It could have stayed that way too, if it hadn't been for a man named William C. Durant. Whoever would have guessed that a carriage maker would buy Cadillac, Oldsmobile, Buick, Pontiac, and Chevrolet, only to form a company called General Motors? As if that wasn't bad enough, he went and invented the electric starter. What was wrong with using a hand-crank to start a car? Good exercise, if you ask me! (*looks disgusted and turns the key to start the car, grimacing as if merely turning the key is too simple a way to start a car*)

William Durant: (*seated in what could be a car, facing Henry Ford*) It wasn't just the starter, Henry. Sure, you made the least expensive car on the market, and cost was certainly important to lots of people, but you forgot about style and comfort. You kept cranking out those plain Tin Lizzies while our Chevrolet, at a higher price, outsold Ford in 1927. The Model T was a good try, but soon General Motors dominated automobile sales.

ACT VI

Cast of Characters
Narrator
Walter Chrysler
Teenage Driver 1
Teenage Driver 2

Props
2 chairs

Narrator: By the 1920s, only the large manufacturers that could make and sell many cars quickly were able to stay in business. The number of U.S. automakers dropped. Gradually, three huge companies took over the manufacturing of most American cars: General Motors, Ford, and Chrysler. Meet Walter Chrysler.

Walter Chrysler: Ford and GM were so worried about each other that they didn't even notice when I bought Dodge, DeSoto, and Plymouth. Of course, GM was still tough to beat. We never could top Chevrolet sales. GM brought in a new man, Alfred Sloan. According to him, Ford was putting people on roads, but GM was enticing them to get fancier wheels. That's when cars got longer, lower, wider, and more powerful. People loved their automobiles!

Teenage Driver 1 (TD 1): (leaning on chair as if leaning on the side of a car) I look cool hanging out near the corner drugstore with my dad's car. I've got a car with an automatic transmission.

Teenage Driver 2 (TD 2): (leaning on chair is if leaning on the side of a car) I look more cool hanging out near the corner drugstore with my dad's car. I have an automatic transmission AND an AM/FM radio.

TD 1: Well, I've got automatic transmission, AM/FM radio, AND power brakes.

TD 2: Oh, yeah? Well, I've got automatic transmission, AM/FM radio, power brakes, AND power steering.

TD 1: So what?! I've got automatic transmission, AM/FM radio, power brakes, power steering, AND tinted windows.

TD 2: Big deal! I've got automatic transmission, AM/FM radio, power brakes, power steering, tinted windows, AND air conditioning.

TD 1: Big whoop! I've got automatic transmission, AM/FM radio, power brakes, power steering, tinted windows, air conditioning, AND my dad's credit card that I can use any time I want to put gas in the car.

TD 2: OK, you win! (*both drivers get in imaginary cars and drive away*)

ACT VII

Cast of Characters
Narrator
Businesswoman
Modern Wife
Modern Husband

Narrator: For many years, the United States produced more cars than all other countries combined. Now, it makes about a third of the world's automobiles. The big three—GM, Ford, and Chrysler—now have to compete with foreign car manufacturers.

Businesswoman: Hold on, there. That's not such a bad thing. Competition brings out the best in business. Thanks to the foreign car industry, we learned to save one of our limited natural resources, oil. After Americans started buying foreign cars that got good gas mileage, the American automobile industry stopped trying to make the longest, shiniest, fastest cars and started trying to make smaller, lighter cars that used less fuel. With foreign cars being sold and repaired by Americans in our country, and the fact that families continue to have second, third, and even fourth cars, there seems to be enough business for everyone.

Modern Wife: (*looking at checkbook and speaking to husband*) You know, with my new promotion, we can afford to pay off William Junior's car and buy a fourth car so that Tracey can have one, too. What do you think?

Modern Husband: (*looking a bit surprised*) I think paying off Junior's car is a great idea, but I'm not so sure Tracey needs a car.

Modern Wife: (*looking annoyed*) Are you saying a boy should have a car, but a girl shouldn't?

Husband: (*looking annoyed*) No, dear, I'm not saying that. It's just that Tracey is only 9. It seems we could wait a while longer, don't you think?

Narrator: Cars already go faster than the law allows, and there are automobiles to suit just about anyone's personality and budget. That leaves only two other areas to conquer in the story of the automobile—safety and alternative fuels for a cleaner environment. Hybrids are gaining in popularity, and even the electric car is getting another look. It will be exciting to see what the next 100 years bring. We've come a long way since the wheel was invented!

Penny for Your Thoughts . . .

What do you think you will be driving when you are a teenager? When you're 40? When you're 60? What will your grandchildren drive?

FAMOUS FOLKS

Pre-Reading Suggestions:

Assessing Prior Knowledge

✦ This play is entitled "Famous Folks." Ask students what makes someone famous. What is the difference between famous and infamous?

✦ Challenge students to list as many famous people as they can in 10 minutes (have students work with partners or small groups, and adjust the time limit as appropriate for different age levels). Next, have students place each famous person listed in categories, such as athletes, scientists, entertainers, and the like.

Post-Reading Suggestions:

Expressing Ideas in Writing

✦ Have students work in small groups to rewrite the ending of the play. Encourage them to share their creations with the group.

✦ Invite students to use the Famous Folks Independent Research sheet as a guide to help them add another character to this play.

✦ Ask students what famous folks, living or dead, they would invite to have lunch with them, and ask why they chose these famous people. Have students write a skit or a play with the dialogue that might happen around a table during such a meeting.

Vocabulary Development

✦ Have students list new words they learned from this play.

Timelines

✦ Challenge students to create a timeline that includes all of the people in the "Famous Folks" play.

FAMOUS FOLKS INDEPENDENT RESEARCH

Directions:

Select a famous person to research. Read at least one biography, and research one additional source. Use the following research form.

Famous person: _____

Why is this person famous? _____

_____

_____

What is unique about this person? _____

_____

_____

When did this person live? _____

Script to be inserted in the Reader's Theater: _____

_____

_____

Where should the script be inserted, and how will it connect to the flow of

the play?_____

_____

_____

_____

_____

FAMOUS FOLKS

Cast of Characters

Student 1	Troy Aikman
Student 2	Michael Jordan
George Washington	Jane and Ann Taylor
Martha Washington	Elvis Presley
Benjamin Franklin	Florence Nightingale
Thomas Edison	Robert Goddard
George Washington Carver	Neil Armstrong
Johnny Appleseed	Ulysses S. Grant
Maria Tallchief	Robert E. Lee
Shaun White	Abraham Lincoln
Lance Armstrong	

Setting
After school waiting to be picked up by parents

Optional Props
Signs worn by actors to identify their characters

Student 1: (*walks out grumbling, holding three biography books*)

Student 2: What are you grumbling about?

Student 1: Well, I got a "B" in spelling today, my peanut butter sandwich was stale, and as if that wasn't bad enough, _____ (teacher's name) said we have to read three biographies!

Student 2: What's wrong with biographies? I LOVE them!

Student 1: You've got to be kidding! (*George and Martha Washington enter behind Student 2's back*) You like reading about old, boring people?

George: Excuse me, young man. (*tapping student on the shoulder*) Who are you calling boring?

Martha: (*looking annoyed*) And OLD?

Student 1: (*looking at other student a little cautiously*) Where did they come from?

Student 2: Your imagination, of course. This happens to me all the time.

George: Don't try to change the subject, young man. What did you mean, boring? (*pauses, then faces audience in an arrogant manner*) Didn't you know I was the first President of the United States, was the Commander-in-Chief of the American Army, was responsible for the first census ever taken, was creator of the National Bank, and am called "The Father of this Country"?

Martha: Don't forget the cherry tree incident.

George: (*embarrassed*) Martha, you know that's not really true. (*becomes arrogant again*) And besides all that, they built a monument to me and named the capital after me—and don't forget the George Washington birthday sales in February!

Martha: Yes, but your picture is only on the one-dollar bill. (*looks sarcastically at audience*) And we all know how far THAT goes nowadays!

George: Martha!

Student 2: Excuse me, but do you know any other famous folks you could introduce us to?

Martha: Sure, we know lots of them. Who would you like to meet?

Both Students: (*look at each other and shake their heads, unable to decide*)

Martha: How about Benjamin Franklin? (*looking at George*) He was an inventor, a philosopher, an author, an editor, a diplomat, AND a humorist.

George: (*looks jealous, rolls eyes*)

Martha: (*calls offstage*) Oh, Ben . . .

Ben: (*walks out eating a large loaf of unsliced bread with another loaf under his arm*) Hi, Lady Washington, George. Looks like a storm's brewing—great day for flying a kite!

Martha: (*excited*) Ben, tell the children here how you invented the lightning rod.

Ben: (*shyly*) Oh, Martha, you know what I always say: "God helps them that help themselves."

(*the Washingtons take a seat*)

Student 2: Mr. Franklin, you sure did a lot of things in your lifetime.

Ben: Well, as I always say, "Never leave that till tomorrow which you can do today." Would you like to meet another inventor?

Student 1: Sure!

Ben: Tom! Thomas Edison, come on out here and meet _____ (Student 1's name) and _____ (Student 2's name).

Tom: Hi, Ben. (*shake hands*) Hello, _____ (Student 1's name) and _____ (Student 2's name).

Ben: Well, I have to go now. As I always say, "Early to bed and early to rise makes a man healthy, wealthy, and wise." (*leaves yawning and eating bread*)

Tom: Which invention would you like me to show you?

Student 1: How about the electric light bulb?

Tom: Oh, that's all anybody cares about. How about my first invention, the electric vote recorder?

Student 2: No, the light bulb.

Tom: Nobody liked my vote counter. (*looks sad, then brightens*) How about my telegraph, mimeograph, dictating machine, electric pen, motion picture camera, projector, ticker-tape machine . . . ?

Student 2: (*shaking head*) No, the light bulb.

Tom: (*gives up, takes bulb out of coat pocket*) I know, I know, the light bulb.

(*phone rings*)

Tom: (*reaches into pocket and pulls out cell phone*) Excuse me, hello . . . Sure, I'll be right there, Alexander. See you kids—gotta run—Mr. Bell wants to talk to me about some new invention of his. I think I saw George Washington Carver coming down the road, though. He was an inventor, too. (*walks off*)

Carver: (*walks in*) Hello, children. Sorry to hear about your peanut butter sandwich being stale, _____ (Student 1's name). Here—(*reaches into pocket and pulls out sandwich*) I always carry an extra with me.

Student 1: (*looking a little skeptical*) Gee, thanks!

Carver: Sure. You know . . . I found almost 300 uses for the common peanut. Funny . . . I never got as much attention as former President Jimmy Carter, and all he did was grow them.

Student 1: Besides being famous for your work in the laboratory, weren't you also a well-known painter and poet?

Carver: Why yes, I was. Do you like to paint and write poetry?

Student 2: Yes, very much.

Carver: Well, I have to go now. I'm working on the soybean.

Student 1 and 2: Bye—good luck with the soybean.

Martha: Talking about all that food has made me hungry. I could use a bit of nourishment.

Appleseed: (*skips in*) At your service, ma'am! John Chapman's the name—call me Johnny—and apples are my game. (*hands everyone an apple*) You can make pies, tarts, jam, jelly, pudding, applesauce, or dumplings, (*looking at audience*) Of course, I like 'em raw. (*takes big bite and skips off*)

Student 1: (*looking at apple*) I'm really beginning to like famous people.

Maria: (*comes spinning out*) I'm Maria Tallchief. The first American ballerina to gain international fame, I showed the world that American Ballet could equal European dancing in quality! (*goes dancing off*)

Shaun: And I'm Shaun White. (*pauses for applause*) Well, some of you may not know me, but they call me "The Flying Tomato." I'm a snowboarding and skateboarding phenom, holding numerous medals from the summer and winter X Games and the 2006 and 2010 Olympics.

Lance: (*bikes out wearing a bright yellow shirt and wrist band*) I'm Lance Armstrong, winner of seven Tour de France competitions. Good luck in the next Olympics, Shaun. Believe me, I know what kind of pressure you'll be under, since you'll be the man to beat. The intensity will be unbearably stressful, but you can handle it.

Shaun: Hey, thanks!

Student 2: Oh, yes. (*getting excited*) I recognize you. You overcame a huge medical issue that almost took your life.

Lance: Yes, I was diagnosed with cancer, but I got the help I needed and am cancer-free now. I started the Lance Armstrong Foundation, where we say unity is strength, knowledge is power, and attitude is everything. LIVE STRONG! (*rides off as students wave goodbye*)

Student 2: Who would you like to . . .

Student 1: Hey, it's Troy Aikman, famous quarterback for the Dallas Cowboys and member of the Football Hall of Fame.

Troy: (*shyly*) Oh, I wouldn't say famous, exactly, but you might have seen me on television as a sports announcer.

Student 2: Oh yes, of course—and you're also known for all your philanthropic work with children.

Student 1: (*speaking to Student 2*) What is philanthropic work?

Student 2: Charity work and generosity.

Student 1: Way cool, man!

Troy: If you want to meet a real legend in sports, you need to meet this next guest in your imagination. (*Michael Jordan comes out dribbling basketball*) Hi, Michael! (*high-fives Michael and walks off stage*)

Michael: Hey, Troy. (*points to shoes*) Nice Air Jordans! (*basketball bounces out of control, bumps Martha*)

Martha: (*screams and runs from ball*) Get that thing away from me! George, who is that person? (*points to Michael*)

Michael: I hold the NBA record for scoring in double-digits in the most consecutive games, I'm a five-time NBA Most Valuable Player and a six-time NBA Finals MVP, I've been selected as one of the greatest players in NBA history, I'm a member of six Chicago Bulls NBA Championships—shall I go on?

George: Very impressive. I just have one question, though.

Michael: Shoot.

George: What is this "NBA"?

Michael: (*walks off shaking his head in disbelief*)

Jane and Ann: Hello, _____ (Student 1's name). (*wave and walk to center stage*)

Student 1: Well, hello, Ann. Hello, Jane. (*turns to Student 1*) This is Jane and Ann Taylor.

Student 2: I never heard of them.

Student 1: They're famous for writing children's poetry.

Student 2: Still haven't heard of them. What poems did they write?

Student 1: Let me give you a hint. They wrote a poem about a star, and you have probably heard it a thousand times.

Student 2: (*stands at attention and salutes*) Oh, of course—"The Star Spangled Banner"!

Student 1: (*laughing*) No, silly, that was Sir Frances Scott Key. The Taylor sisters wrote "Twinkle, Twinkle, Little Star."

Jane and Ann: (*reciting*) Twinkle, twinkle, little star. (**hold star overhead**)
  How I wonder what you are!
  Up above the world so high,
  Like a diamond in the sky.

  When the blazing sun is gone,
  When he nothing shines upon,
  Then you show your little light
  Twinkle, twinkle, all the night.

  Bye, now! (**wave as they leave**)

Martha: Since we are speaking of literature, why don't we meet some famous figures from music? Chopin, Mozart, Beethoven—the list is endless.

Student 2: Wow! There are so many. It would take all day to meet them all. Why don't we meet one of the most famous musicians of all?

George: (*to Martha*) Care to dance, my dear?

Martha: Thank you, I'd love to. (**they begin waltzing**)

Student 2: (*shouting as Elvis enters*) ELVIS PRESLEY!

Elvis: (*comes out, lifts one side of top lip, wiggles one leg*)

Martha: (*swoons, George helps her to her chair*)

Elvis: I often have that effect on women! (**sings one verse of song, throws scarf to audience, waves to fans as he leaves**)

Florence: (*holding lamp in hand, rushes over to Martha*) Lady Washington, are you all right?

George: I think she'll be fine. She's just had a terrible shock.

Florence: I am Florence Nightingale, founder of modern methods of nursing. Yes, I could see she was suffering terribly.

George: Oh?

Florence: Yes, you may have heard me referred to as "the lady with the lamp." I got this name by carrying a lamp on my hospital rounds.

Students 2: Miss Nightingale, weren't you also a women's rights activist?

Florence: If you mean to ask if I worked for equal rights for women, you can bet your bloomers I did.

Martha: (*regains consciousness, but faints again when she hears the word bloomers*) Oh!

Florence: Well, I must go now and tend to more patients.

Student 2: That sure was exciting. (*Goddard starts walking out, looking down at the rocket model in his hands*) Oh, here comes someone else very exciting.

Student 1: Who is he?

Student 2: I'm surprised you don't know him. He's "The Father of the Modern Rocket."

Goddard: Yes, I guess you could say I got the space program "off the ground." (*pauses, waiting for laughter*) Well, I always was better at science than comedy. Let me introduce you to a man who has been very involved in the modern-day space program, Astronaut Neil Armstrong.

Armstrong: (*comes out*) Nice to see you again, Mr. Goddard. (*they shake hands*) I've always admired your brilliant work.

Goddard: Thank you, and I admired your courage in being the first human to set foot on the moon.

Armstrong: Yes, but without your work, that would have been impossible.

Goddard: Yes, but . . .

Student 2: Gentlemen, please. We appreciate both of you.

Student 1: (*shakes their hands*) Yes, thank you for coming. (*they leave*) I know another pair in history that would be exciting to meet.

Student 2: Great, who are they?

Grant: (*salutes*) General Ulysses S. Grant at your service—Commander in Chief of the Northern armies in the War Between the States and 18th President of the United States of America.

Student 1: Nice to make your acquaintance sir. I was expecting General Robert E. Lee to come out with you.

Grant: Oh, I asked him to come, but he wouldn't. Stubborn pride!

Student 2: (*looking offstage*) General Lee . . .

Lee: (*answering from offstage, where he cannot be seen*) He's not here!

Student 2: Please come out, General Lee.

Lee: NO!

Student 2: But why, sir?

Lee: The South lost the war between the States, and I had to surrender to Grant.

Student 1: That's OK, General Lee. We know you were a great leader and did the best you could under the circumstances. Besides, it really worked out for the best.

Lee: (*peeking around and coming out slowly*) Really?

Grant: Sure, Bob. Now, all Americans are free, and all the states are united.

Lee: Gee . . . I guess you're right. Plus, if I hadn't surrendered, who knows? We may never have had baseball, hot dogs, apple pie . . .

Grant: (*patting him on the back*) We get the point. Sounds like you're hungry—let's go have some chicken fried steak and biscuits dripping in gravy. The South always did have the best darn food! (*they walk off together*)

Student 1: Well, I'm sure glad that had a happy ending.

George: Excuse me, but it seems to me you still haven't met anyone else who comes up to my . . . shall we say . . . standards.

Student 1: That may be true, General Washington, but there is one more person I'd like _____ (Student 2's name) to meet.

George: Oh, and who might that be?

Abe: Hello, George. Sorry I missed your birthday. Happy birthday.

George: Why, Abe, how good to see you! Happy birthday to you, too.

Abe: I understand you're trying to decide who is the most famous historical figure?

George: Well, Abe, I've got to admit, you sure did a lot for this country. And you do have a mighty nice monument in Washington, DC, and we can't forget your face being on the . . . penny. (*covers face and snickers*)

Abe: Yes, I'm mighty proud of my face being on the penny. I saved every penny I made, and I tried to tighten the nation's pocketbook while I served as President. As far as there being a single most famous person, though, I'm not sure there is one. We make each other great. Don't you agree, George?

(*Martha nudges George to make him agree*)

George: Yes, Abe, I'm sure you are right.

(*action freezes*)

Student 2: Well, _____ (Student 1's name). How do you feel about biographies now?

Student 1: Are you kidding? I LOVE them! Let's go back to the library.

(*everyone returns to thunderous applause*)

Optional: Have the entire cast sing "The Star-Spangled Banner" or another appropriate song.

Penny for Your Thoughts . . .

Who is your favorite character in this play? Which other historical characters would you have included, and why?

ZANY ZONES

Pre-Reading Suggestions:

Assessing Prior Knowledge
- Create a K-W-L chart. Ask students to fill in the first two columns of the chart. What do they already know about the zones of the ocean? What would they like to know about the zones of the ocean?
- Challenge students to write about the kind of sea creature they would most like to be and where they think this creature would live in the ocean.

Post-Reading Suggestions:

Drawing Conclusions
- Have students help fill in the remaining column on the K-W-L chart. Ask students what they learned about the ocean zones.

Expressing Ideas in Writing
- Have students work in small groups to rewrite the ending to the play. Allow time for groups to share.
- Have students revisit their writing from the pre-reading activity. Ask them to revise their writing by telling about the ocean zone in which they would live.

Vocabulary Development
- Ask students to list new words they have learned from this play.

Research
- Challenge students to draw and then identify the five zones of the ocean, and then list or draw some of the plants and animals that can be found in each zone.
- Have students choose three of the following activities to complete:
  - List the five oceans on Earth in order from smallest to largest.
  - List the five oceans on Earth from shallowest to deepest.
  - State the differences between oceans and seas. Name at least 10 seas.
  - Find out how much of the Earth's surface is covered by oceans.

- ✦ Describe and explain the many functions oceans serve on Earth.
- ✦ Make a mobile that demonstrates the diverse web of life in the ocean.

ZANY ZONES

Cast of Characters

Zooplankton 1
Zooplankton 2
Phytoplankton 1
Phytoplankton 2
Jellyfish
Herring
Whale
Giant Ray
Squid
Butterfly Fish

Octopus
Sea Cucumber
Sea Star
Tube Worm
Crab
Lobster
Clam 1
Clam 2
Clam 3
Snail

Setting

Ocean

Optional Props

Signs worn to identify sea
creatures
Blue bed sheet to make waves

Zooplankton 1: I know you keep telling me we are the most important animals in the ocean, but what good is that when nobody can see us?

Zooplankton 2: It doesn't matter that we are so tiny people can't see us. We are the most important link in the food web, and we get to live in the sunlight zone. We have privacy, not like those celebrity dolphins, and that's good.

Phytoplankton 1: I beg your pardon! Everyone knows that plant plankton, not animal plankton, is the basic food of the ocean. That makes US the most important link in the food web.

Phytoplankton 2: Don't pay any attention to them. They are always bragging. It makes them feel better about themselves. It's no fun being called "shrimp" all your life. Shrimp! (*pause*) See, it hurts.

Jellyfish: I can't believe what I'm hearing! We are all part of the plankton classification. We are known as the floaters and the drifters. Not a terribly distinguished description, if you want my opinion.

Herring: Come on, here come the drifters again.

Whale: Eat, eat, eat! That's all you ever do!

Herring: That's all I do? That's all you do, too!

Giant Ray: Do you have any idea how much plankton you guys have to eat to get one good meal? Why don't you eat fish, like some of the other sea creatures in the nekton classification?

Zooplankton 2: Disgusting. I never eat anything with a face. I guess that makes me a vegan.

Squid: What's a vegan? More importantly, what are nekton? Does that include me?

Butterfly Fish: Yes, that includes you and all of the other animals that can swim freely in water without the help of currents. Most of us live in the upper zones of the ocean, but we can be found in all of the zones.

Octopus: Look out! Here comes another member of the family! Shark! (*sings* Jaws *theme song*)

Sea Cucumber: Do you mind? You are stepping on me! Just look at me. I am less cucumber-y now.

Sea Star: Oops! Sorry, old man. No disrespect meant. You just kind of blend in with the ocean floor, that's all.

Tube Worm: Many of the creatures that live on the bottom blend in. I'm an exception. I stand out, and as you can see, I have a very striking color. It's OK, you can look. Take a picture if you like.

Crab: You think you're so great! You may be attractive, but what kind of protection do you have?

Lobster: Don't mind him, he's just crabby. Get it? Crabby! See, he's a crab, and I said crabby. That's a pun!

Clam 1: We get it. It's just not that funny. Do you guys mind? We're trying to get some sleep down here.

Clam 2: We've had a terrible day! Divers collected several members of our family today!

Clam 3: It's tragic! We need you to give us a break and clam up! Hey, Lobster, did you get that one?

Snail: All of you benthos creatures better clam up. Here come more divers and a submersible.

FOUNDERS OR PARTNERS?

Pre-Reading Suggestions:

Vocabulary Development
+ Have students define "founder." Have students compare "founder" with "partner."

Assessing Prior Knowledge
+ Ask students if they know the founders of their city, county, or country. Have them list as many founders as possible.
+ Ask students to explain their understanding of veterinary medicine and why they think it is important.

Post-Reading Suggestions:

Inferences
+ Ask students how they think researchers in human medicine and surgical techniques could benefit from collaborating with researchers in veterinary medicine, and vice versa.

Research
+ Challenge students to locate specific examples of how human and veterinary branches of medicine have benefited from each other in recent years.
+ Challenge students to discover founders (or "fathers" and "mothers") in other fields or movements, such as religion, civil rights, sports, music, and art. They should present this information in a creative format, such as a song, mural, skit, or diorama.

FOUNDERS OR PARTNERS?

Note to Teacher

✦ This short skit explores the relationship and partnership between two little-known men who are credited with creating the foundation of veterinary medicine.

Cast of Characters

Aspyrtus (serious and strict man)
Vegetius (funny without realizing it)

Optional Props

2 sheets for togas

Aspyrtus: Greetings from the past—as in, more than 2,000 years ago. My name is Aspyrtus, and I'm known as the Father of Veterinary Medicine.

Vegetius: So I guess that makes me the mother? Excuse me, but I thought we were known as the FOUNDERS of Veterinary Medicine.

Aspyrtus: Well, it depends on what book you read. Oh, how rude of me. Let me introduce my partner, Vegetius, here all the way from the Byzantine Empire. We worked together to write the first detailed guide for veterinarians. It was a bestseller for many years.

Vegetius: (*pointing to partner, and with great pride*) You see, Aspyrtus was the leading veterinarian of his day and personally described many of the medical and surgical problems associated with the horse and the cow. I was never an actual veterinarian, myself. I was just very good at writing down details, adding drawings, and expanding on the comments made by my esteemed colleague.

Aspyrtus: Yes, expanding on my comments. (*looks disgusted*) Anyway, I think we are getting ahead of ourselves. I believe we are here to enlighten these youth on the history of veterinary medicine.

Vegetius: Very well. You begin, and I will expand.

Aspyrtus: (*sarcastically*) Gee, thanks! Before human beings were "civilized," they viewed animals, all animals, as sources of food and clothing. They even moved from place to place to follow them.

Vegetius: It was eat or be eaten!

Aspyrtus: Thank you. Eventually, humankind began to stay in one place and grow crops. That is when they began domesticating animals. They discovered that some animals, such as horses and oxen, could help them with work.

Vegetius: They also discovered it was much easier to raise their own meat than to chase after it.

Aspyrtus: That's where veterinarians came in. People started realizing that they needed to keep their animals healthy.

Vegetius: Still, veterinarians didn't get a lot of respect or attention. Take Aspyrtus, for example . . . He wasn't really appreciated until he was gone.

Aspyrtus: That's true. The medical profession was more concerned with its own growth than with the care of livestock.

Vegetius: It took some terrible plagues, with millions of animals and humans dying, before people took veterinary medicine seriously. I guess that's understandable.

Aspyrtus: That's when sick animals were finally isolated from healthy animals and keeping animals in clean environments took hold.

Vegetius: Medical doctors also saw how some diseases in animals could affect the health of humans.

Aspyrtus: So they finally began working together.

Vegetius: Hurrah for veterinarians! (*does victory dance, confetti falls down*)

Aspyrtus: Thank you, Vegetius.

Vegetius: I meant ALL veterinarians.

Aspyrtus: Whatever!

Penny for Your Thoughts . . .

Imagine if the field of veterinary medicine had never been developed. What problems could have evolved from the absence of veterinary medicine?

THEY CALL IT CIRCULATION

Pre-Reading Suggestions:

Assessing Prior Knowledge
✦ Ask students to tell you as much as they already know about the circulatory system. What does it do? What organs are involved? How does it work?

Research
✦ Have students research, diagram, label, and explain the circulatory system.

Synthesis
✦ Have students use the information they have learned about the circulatory system to simulate or dramatize the process.

Post-Reading Suggestions:

Writing
✦ Have students add more speaking parts to the Reader's Theater.
✦ Have students interject more humor in the script.
✦ Instead of using the suggested song in the play, have students create their own theme song for the circulatory system.

Persuasive Writing
✦ In this Reader's Theater, the Heart continually says that it is the most important part of the circulatory system. Have students write a paragraph agreeing or disagreeing that the Heart is the most important organ in the entire body.

Creative Writing
✦ Have students write a Reader's Theater about one of the other systems of the body.

THEY CALL IT CIRCULATION

Note to Teacher

✦ There are 19 parts in this play. Red Blood Cells 3, 4, and 5 only speak in unison. White Blood Cells 4 and 5 only speak in unison. The Heart has the biggest part and should be assigned to a strong reader. Assign parts, then let students practice reading, first silently, and then to a partner. Avoid asking students to read aloud without time to practice.

Cast of Characters

News Reporter
Heart
5 Red Blood Cells
5 White Blood Cells
Plasma
Right Atrium (auricle)

Right Ventricle
Lungs
Left Atrium (auricle)
Left Ventricle
Germ

Setting

Television news station

Optional Props

Water guns for white blood cells
Red balls
Paper wads to represent CO2
Trash cans to dispose of CO2

Construction paper sword for germ
CD with song "We Got the Beat"

News Reporter: Hello! I'm _____ (Student name), reporting for _____ (Name of local news station). Today we are going to go on location to the center of the body's circulatory system—the heart. The heart is an amazing muscle. It's like the Energizer bunny—it keeps going and going and going. It is the only muscle in your body that never takes a rest. Your heart is about the size of your first. The average adult heart beats about 70 times a minute. For more information, let's go to the source.

Heart: Thank you, _____ (Name of news reporter). Let me begin by saying that I am not shaped like a Valentine's Day heart. The greeting card companies have made it very difficult for hearts like me to be recognized in public. And you were right: I am a muscle, and I never get to take a vacation! How would you like to go through life without a vacation? It's a good thing I'm in such good shape! My main job is to pump blood throughout the body. Blood has—

All Blood Cells: Hey, Heart! We're here, too! If you get to tell your story, so do we!

Heart: Oh, all right. Even though I am the major attraction, the head honcho, the big cheese, so to speak, of the circulatory system, I suppose I could let you tell your story.

Red Blood Cell 1: Without us, Heart, you would be out of a job!

All Blood Cells: Yeah, right on!

White Blood Cell 1: We fight germs. We don't just fight them—we destroy them!

White Blood Cells: Yay! Destroy the germs! Who needs 'em?!

White Blood Cell 2: Hey, we can't forget about the platelets. Platelets float around in the blood, too. They are little, jagged cells. When you cut your finger, the platelets get caught on the edges of the cut and make sticky threads to help stop the bleeding. The sticky thread that comes out helps your cuts to form blood clots. Of course, all of the cells depend on something else to get us easily through the body.

Heart: Ah . . . and that would be me. So I'll get back to telling my story . . .

Plasma: No, Heart, they are talking about me, Plasma. I make up more than half of what is considered blood. I carry nutrients to the body along with all of the red and white blood cells. You can think of me as the river that carries the cells along. Now, though, we DO need to go back to the heart.

Heart: Thanks, Plasma. Now that you've heard about the blood, you need to hear a lot more about me—(*pause*) because I AM the most important star in the circulatory system.

All Others: Oh, please! (*groan, moan, shake heads*)

Red Blood Cell 2: Heart, just remember that without us, you wouldn't have a job. All of the systems of the body depend upon each other. Without blood, YOU wouldn't have anything to PUMP or PUSH around!

Heart: OK. You made your point! I guess I need to tell you about what's on the inside of me. I'm not just a solid muscle on the inside. You can think of me as a four-bedroom house. I even have doors between my bedrooms that are called valves. As I pump, the valves open and close, allowing my friends—the red and white blood cells, platelets, and plasma—to tour my house.

Each room, or chamber, in my house has a name. Let me introduce my chambers. Please meet Right Atrium, Right Ventricle, Left Atrium, and Left Ventricle.

Right Atrium: Hello. (*waving to camera*) I'm Right Atrium. When the blood enters the heart, I am the first chamber it comes to. I receive blood that is carrying waste called carbon dioxide. After blood leaves me, it goes to my friend, Right Ventricle.

Right Ventricle: I'm Right Ventricle. I am stronger than Right Atrium, because I have the job of pumping blood into the lungs. While in the lungs, the red blood cells drop off carbon dioxide and pick up oxygen.

Lungs: I'm Lungs. I'm a part of the respiratory system. Without me, the circulatory system would not have a job, and vice versa. All systems in the body depend upon one another for survival. The heart and blood depend on me to supply them with oxygen. They also depend on me to get rid of carbon dioxide. The blood comes from the right ventricle, drops off carbon dioxide, and picks up oxygen.

Left Atrium: And then it comes to me, Left Atrium. I receive the blood that contains oxygen, and then I pass it on to Left Ventricle.

Left Ventricle: As Left Ventricle, it's my job to pump the blood to the rest of the body. I am stronger than Left Atrium, but as a chamber, I realize that each chamber of the heart depends upon the others to do their jobs. The rest of the body depends on me to keep it supplied with blood.

Heart: Once the blood leaves me, it travels through tunnels called blood vessels. There are three kinds of blood vessels: arteries, veins, and capillaries. Arteries carry blood away from me. Veins carry blood back to me. Capillaries are tiny vessels that carry blood to tiny places in the body. With all of this traveling, you would think that blood takes a long time to go through the whole body. But amazingly, the entire journey of blood from the heart, through the body, and back to me only takes about 23 seconds.

News Reporter: Would you say that again? That's incredible!

Heart: Yes, of course. I am pretty incredible. The entire journey of blood—from the heart, through the body, and back to me, the heart—takes about 23 seconds.

Allow us to demonstrate how the blood flows through the heart, lungs, and body.

(*Atriums, Ventricles, and Lungs take their positions; Blood Cells begin circulation; White Cells carry water guns; Red Cells carry oxygen, dispose of oxygen, pick up carbon dioxide, and then exchange carbon dioxide for more oxygen in Lungs*)

While the cells are circulating, play the song "We Got the Beat"

(*after three or four circulations, Germ enters, screaming and waving his or her sword, trying to destroy the blood cells*)

Germ: OK, you sorry cells! I'm here to spread disease and make everyone sick! SICK! SICK! SICK! And nobody can stop me! I am unstoppable! I am Germ! Hear me ROAR! (*makes a loud roar sound*)

White Blood Cells: Attack! Destroy! Let's get him!

Germ: Hey! That's not fair. There are so many of you. AAAAHHHH! (*goes down swinging his sword as White Blood Cells squirt him with water guns*)

Germ: (*very dramatic death scene*) AAAHHHHHH! I'm dying! Dying! Oh, White Blood Cells! Look what you've done to me! You wretched Cells! You've destroyed all of my lovely, evil work! Dying! Dying! OOOHHHHH!

All: Yay! Hooray! No more Germ! You did it! Let's hear it for the White Blood Cells!

White Blood Cell 3: We couldn't have done it without all of you! All of the cells in the body depend upon the rest of the body to do its job so that they can do theirs. We all destroyed the Germ!

All: (*wild cheering*) Hip, hip, hooray!

News Reporter: And that is the story of the circulatory system, as told by the experts on location. This is _____ (Student name), reporting very much alive from _____ (Name of local news station). Thank you for watching.

ZEUS SUMMONS THE GREEK GODS AND GODDESSES

Pre-Reading Suggestions:

Assessing Prior Knowledge
✦ Have students tell you what they already know about Greek mythology.

Prediction
✦ Have students read the title and predict why they think Zeus might be summoning his primary gods and goddesses.

Post-Reading Suggestions:

Reading Comprehension
✦ Have students list the Greek gods and goddesses in the play. They should use what they learned in the Reader's Theater to write what each of the characters is responsible for.

Vocabulary Development
✦ Many words in this Reader's Theater contain Latin roots. See if students can find the words that go with the following roots:
  ◇ **civ** means citizen
  ◇ **grat** means thank, please
  ◇ **multi(i)** means many, much
  ◇ **jus** means law
  ◇ **per** means thoroughly

Independent Research
✦ Have students research the major Roman gods and goddesses. Compare and contrast the main characters with the Greek gods and goddesses.

Expressing Ideas in Writing
✦ Have students write a dialogue between Hera and Aphrodite that might have taken place following the end of the meeting.

ZEUS SUMMONS THE GREEK GODS AND GODDESSES

Note to Teacher

✦ Assign parts, then let students practice reading, first silently and then to a partner. Avoid asking students to read aloud without time to practice.

Cast of Characters

Seasons	Athena
Poseidon	Hephaestus
Hades	Artemis
Hermes	Demeter
Zeus	Hestia
Hera	Aphrodite
Apollo	
Ares	

Setting

The palace on Mount Olympus, located in a mysterious region far above the Earth over the highest mountain in Greece

Optional Props

Signs worn by actors to identify them

Seasons: (*in a loud, firm voice*) Halt, who goes there at the gate?

Poseidon: (*in a very loud, firm voice*) It is I, Poseidon, ruler of the seas and brother of Zeus.

Seasons: (*cautious*) How do I know it is really you, and not just some imposter?

Poseidon: (*loud and angry*) If you don't let me in, you might see just how sharp my three-pronged spear is.

Seasons: (*scared and apologetic*) Oh, I'm sorry, sir, I didn't see the trident. Please come in. Your brother, supreme ruler of the gods, is waiting for you.

Poseidon: (*annoyed and impatient*) What is this about? I have a vast empire to take care of myself, you know.

Seasons: (*still scared and apologetic*) Sorry, sir. I don't have any idea. But he has been throwing lightning bolts all morning, so he is not in the best of moods.

Hades: (*in an evil voice*) Yes, I have heard that racket. It was loud enough to wake the dead.

Poseidon: (*not very pleased to see Hades*) Oh, hello, Hades. So, our brother summons us? What could it be about?

Hades: (*annoyed*) How should I know? I'm busy ruling the underworld and the dead. I know it is relatively quiet down there, but I have a lot of souls on my plate. Busy, busy, busy.

Seasons: (*still scared*) Excuse me, sirs, but Zeus and Hera are seated on their thrones, awaiting you in the Council Hall.

Hermes: (*in a hurried but happy voice*) Better hurry, uncles, Father is waiting. Wish you had sandals and helmets with wings on them, like I do. That way, you could mount your thrones swiftly and wouldn't keep my father waiting.

(*short pause as Poseidon and Hades mount their thrones*)

Zeus: (*in a booming voice*) Let the meeting of the Olympian gods begin!

Hera: (*calmly and sweetly*) Husband, be patient. Poseidon and Hades have traveled a long distance. Let the servants bring them Nectar to drink and Ambrosia to eat.

Zeus: (*angry*) We have no time for hospitality. We have a serious problem.

Hermes: (*friendly but nervous*) Let me get the refreshments. I can do it much faster.

Hades: (*in a low voice*) Showoff!

Poseidon: (*annoyed*) Never mind. I have no appetite—let's get the meeting started.

Zeus: Apollo! Knock off that noise!

Apollo: Father! I am a master musician, and god of light and reason. Why are you so upset?

Zeus: (*less angry*) Sorry, son. We have a problem, and I need the council of all of you to help me solve it.

Ares: (*conceited*) As the god of war and your bravest son, not to mention tallest and most handsome, I am confident that I can wipe out this problem for you at once. (*in evil voice*) And I'll enjoy doing it.

Athena: Let me help you, brother. I sprang from my father's head full-grown and in full armor. I am the protector of civilized life and will fight by your side. I also am wise and can keep a cool head in battle.

Hephaestus: (*to Hera in a pleading voice*) Mother, as the god of fire, I can make all the armor and weapons we need. My weak legs keep me from fighting, but I promise our militia will be well equipped for battle.

Artemis: (*sounding cold and pitiless*) As the moon goddess and bow-and-arrows hunting expert, I will manipulate the light in the night sky so our warriors will have all the advantages. I want our enemies destroyed with no mercy!

Demeter: (*with motherly concern*) Wait, Artemis. Speaking as goddess of the harvest, I wonder if that is really such a good idea. What effects will that have on mothers and their precious children?

Artemis: (*angrily, coldly*) You and your baby have no part in this discussion.

Hestia: (*pleading weakly*) Zeus, my brother, all of this talk is upsetting. How can I be the keeper of hearth and home with all of this conflict?

Zeus: (*loudly*) SILENCE! Our problem is that someone is increasing greenhouse gas emissions. One of you is causing massive climate change!

Hades: (*jealous*) I'm not to blame, but I wish I had thought of that—the hotter the better!

Zeus: (*accusingly*) Is it you, Poseidon? Are you tampering with the atmosphere?

Poseidon: (*loudly, angrily*) I find that accusation offensive! I can't believe you would accuse me of purposely disturbing our perfect world.

Zeus: (*calming down*) Demeter, could your little daughter Persephone have gotten into something she shouldn't have?

Demeter: (*defensively*) You know that would be impossible. I never let Persephone out of my sight, not even for a minute. She sits on my lap even as I speak to you now.

Apollo: (*very calmly*) Father, I am also the god of truth. Let me search the hearts of all the gods and goddesses and see who is causing global warming.

Zeus: (*happy*) Yes, excellent idea—search the hearts and minds of everyone here!

(*long pause*)

Hestia: OK, OK—(*sobbing*) I admit it. I am the only one with no real powers. Goddess of the home and hearth? What is that, anyway? I sit tending a fire day in, day out. Nothing ever changes. I'm just "sister of Zeus." I don't have any statues erected in my image. I don't have an emblem or a symbol. There aren't even any myths written about me.

Zeus: (*shocked*) Hestia!

Hestia: (*unapologetic*) So I caused a few droughts, changed a few ecosystems—what's the harm? At least I finally got out of the house and kept occupied, like all of the rest of you.

Aphrodite: Oh, Hestia. I had no idea you felt that way.

Hestia: Of course you didn't. You just go around looking gorgeous and melting men's hearts. I've even seen you flirting with Zeus. You have no time for anybody else.

Hera: (*threateningly*) I'm sure you are mistaken about Aphrodite flirting with Zeus. Everyone knows what happens when Zeus strays from me. It wouldn't go unpunished.

Aphrodite: (*scared*) Of course I would never flirt with Zeus. Hestia is just trying to change the subject and distract us.

Hades: (*in a low voice*) I always said Hestia was a little "off balance." But this is certainly getting interesting. Well worth the trip from the underworld!

Demeter: You should just accept your position with gratitude, Hestia. It's not like being the goddess of the harvest is all that glamorous.

Hades: You can come to the underworld, my lovely. I can always use your help. We have many souls that keep our fires burning.

Poseidon: (*angrily, ignoring Hades*) Hestia, you were the cause of those problems?

Zeus: (*in loud, angry voice*) SILENCE!

Hera: Husband, more civility, please. Hestia needs help. She is right. She needs to get out more. One of the nymphs can tend the home fires occasionally. She needs a proper domain. She needs a purpose, she needs a myth about her, and for heaven's sake, let's get her a symbol.

Zeus: Well, Hestia? If we do all these things, will you stop increasing the greenhouse gas?

Hestia: (*sincerely apologetic*) Yes, brother. I am sorry for all of the problems I have caused for you and all the other gods and goddesses. I should have come to you and told you how I felt.

Ares: (*anxious and curious*) So what justice will you inflict upon her, mighty Zeus?

(*short pause while Zeus thinks*)

Zeus: (*in strong but not angry voice*) This matter is over! Be gone and bring me some Nectar and a double portion of Ambrosia! I HATE conflict! (***throws lightning bolt***)

ALEXANDER THE GREAT

Pre-Reading Suggestions:

Assessing Prior Knowledge
+ See what students know about Alexander the Great.
+ When was he alive?
+ Where was he during most of his life?
+ What is he known for?

Post-Reading Suggestions:

Expressing Ideas in Writing
+ Alexander was taught that courage and honor counted more than life itself. Have students write a paragraph agreeing or disagreeing with this idea.
+ Have students write about a time when someone told them that they couldn't do something because of their age or size. What happened?

Sequential Order
+ Challenge students to create a timeline for Alexander the Great that lists his accomplishments.

Research
+ Have students look up and locate all of the current cities in the world that still have the name Alexandria. They should plot a map showing where Alexander and his men fought.

Identifying Facts and Details
+ Have students reread the play. Have them write down facts that can be verified and separate them from facts that cannot be verified.

ALEXANDER THE GREAT

Note to Teacher
✦ This is a two-act play. Assign six students to perform Act I and seven students to perform Act II. Have both groups practice, first silently and then aloud. Have the two groups perform for one another.

Cast of Characters

Act I
Narrator 1
Alexander
Stable Master
Narrator 2
King
Narrator 3

Act II
Narrator 1
Narrator 2
Narrator 3
Narrator 4
Geographer
Astronomer
Priest

Setting
Outdoors at a riding stable

Optional Props
Signs worn by actors to identify their characters

ACT I

Narrator 1: The magnificent black stallion reared, throwing the king's stable master to the ground. His assistant shouted at the wild horse, pulling on his halter. King Philip of northern Greece and his 7-year-old son, Alexander, along with many important elders, stood looking on.

Alexander: He's the most beautiful horse I've ever seen. But they are frightening him.

Stable Master: Sire, I beg you not to buy this horse. He is too wild!

Alexander: No! Don't listen! He's a good horse!

Narrator 2: The bearded elders were shocked by Alexander's rudeness.

Alexander: Father! Listen! They don't know how to handle him!

King: Are you telling me my horsemen can't handle horses?

Alexander: No, sir—well, I mean, I think I know how to control him.

Narrator 3: Everybody laughed at Alexander.

King: And after you tame him, will you pay for him?

Alexander: I will somehow!

King: All right. I'll bet you the price of the horse you can't ride him.

Narrator 1: Silent and anxious, everybody watched the young prince. Without hesitation, he ran toward the horse. As he came closer, Alexander's run changed to a slow walk. The great black stallion seemed larger now that Alexander was closer.

Narrator 2: Alexander's heart pounded with fear, but he could not turn back now. He had been taught that courage and honor counted more than life itself.

Narrator 3: Slowly he reached for the reins. He could see that the animal was as frightened as he was. Alexander felt sorry for the horse. Maybe the horse sensed his feelings, because he allowed Alexander to turn him around so that they were facing the sun.

Narrator 1: Alexander lightly swung himself onto the horse's bare back. The stallion leaped forward, powerful hooves pounding the Earth. Alexander bent low, talking softly into the horse's ear while applying just enough pressure to keep him headed into the sun. Gradually the horse grew calmer. Alexander straightened up, laughing joyously. The horse galloped free. Everybody cheered, then Alexander and the beautiful stallion cantered back to his father.

King: Well done, my son! What magic did you use?

Alexander: No magic, Father. He was frightened by his own shadow. I turned him to face into the sun. When he no longer saw his shadow, he was mine.

Narrator 2: This horse and rider cast their shadows across the world. Bucephalus became the most famous horse in history. He never let anyone but Alexander ride him.

Narrator 3: When Alexander was preparing to mount, the noble horse would lower his body to help him on. In battle, Alexander always rode Bucephalus.

ACT II

Narrator 1: King Philip died when Alexander was 20. Alexander became king, and war became his business. He won every battle, even when his army was heavily outnumbered.

Narrator 2: Alexander always led his men into battle wearing a white plume on his helmet for the enemy to see. His men were devoted to him.

Narrator 3: At first, Alexander went to war in order to bring together different areas of Greece. It took him 2 years to do this. Then he marched on to do battle with many other nations and peoples in order to increase his power. Whenever he defeated an area, men from that area joined his army. Before long, instead of having a Greek army, Alexander had an international army.

Narrator 4: For 4 years Alexander marched east, conquering and starting new cities, all named Alexandria. Alexander and his army, who never lost a battle, marched off the map of the known world. The king and his men didn't know where they were. Today we know that they had reached India.

Geographer: We are near the top of the world, where Amazons rule. Beware those mighty women warriors and hunters.

Astronomer: Ahead lies ocean. Beyond its shores, giant serpents hide in the dark sea spray.

Priest: Turn back. Don't make the gods angry. The edge of the Earth, where you are, is forbidden to man.

Narrator 1: But Alexander was Alexander. He pressed on into India. His soldiers were tired of war. They had been fighting for 8 years. They wanted to go back home.

Narrator 2: Still, the army followed where Alexander led. He led them into one of their most difficult battles.

Narrator 3: On the far side of a rain-swollen river, a powerful Indian army waited, blocking Alexander's advance. His army came up against something new and different: a wall of war elephants.

Narrator 4: This strange sight and smell terrified the horses of Alexander's army. Right there on the battlefield, Alexander came up with a plan to use the Indian elephants against the Indians.

Narrator 1: He commanded his archers to shoot the elephant drivers. Then his foot soldiers pressed the Indian soldiers back against the animals. Meanwhile, his archers aimed more arrows at the elephant. Wounded and without drivers, the elephants panicked, trampling their own people as well as Alexander's. The Indian line broke and crumpled in defeat.

Narrator 2: During the battle, Alexander had been riding his famous horse, Bacephalus. Suddenly the magnificent horse trembled, and then fell, lifeless. The strain of the long battle had been too much.

Narrator 3: The great Alexander himself led the funeral procession and buried Bucephalus with military honors. On the burial site, Alexander founded another city. For once, Alexander did not name this city Alexandria. Instead, he called it Bucephala.

Narrator 4: After the capture of India, the rainy season began. Everything was soaked. Metal armor and swords became rusted, clothing and bedding rotted, food turned moldy, bodies grew diseased with sores, and poisonous snakes and clouds of vicious mosquitoes tormented the army. The wet and weary soldiers had no stomach for more war. The army mutinied, refusing to march on.

Narrator 1: Alexander begged his men to continue fighting, but they stood silent, refusing to move. Alexander went to his tent and refused to sleep, eat, change clothes, or speak to anyone.

Narrator 2: After 3 days, realizing that his troops would not give in, Alexander decided to let the gods decide what his next step would be.

Narrator 3: His high priests made sacrifices, read signs, and then made wise decisions.

Priest: The gods do not want you to go any further.

Narrator 4: Alexander and his army accepted this decision, and the army marched back home.

Narrator 1: Alexander never returned to his native Greece. He remained in India, planning new conquests.

Narrator 2: Alexander died from an infection brought on by exhaustion and war wounds. He was 33 years old.

Narrator 3: He had conquered the known world, leaving behind him 70 new cities named Alexandria.

Narrator 4: More important, he unified the world and showed that people of different races and nations could live and work side by side.

THE PERFECT PET

Pre-Reading Suggestions:

Fluency
◆ Challenge students to list as many pets as they can in 10 minutes. Have students work with partners or small groups, and adjust the time limit as appropriate for different age levels.

Categorization
◆ Students should create categories for the pets they listed.

Fact or Opinion
◆ The title of the play is "The Perfect Pet." What do students think would make the perfect pet? Be sure that they distinguish between fact and opinion when giving their answer.

Post-Reading Suggestions:

Drawing Conclusions
◆ Ask students the following question: After reading or listening to this play, can you conclude that cockroaches are in fact the perfect pet? Explain your answer.

Expressing Ideas in Writing
◆ Do the students think Mason really wanted a cockroach for a pet? Have them explain their answers.
◆ Have students add more characters to the play.
◆ Have students write a new ending.

Research
◆ Students should select two facts they learned about cockroaches and do research to verify if the facts, as stated, are true.
◆ The mother in this play recommended that her son, Mason, have a turtle for a pet. Students should list the pros and cons of having a turtle for a pet.

◆ Have students research another unusual animal and rewrite the play using that animal or insect as the point of contention between the mother and child.

Vocabulary Development
◆ Have students list new words they learned from this play.

Facts and Details
◆ Have students illustrate one of the scenes in the play, paying careful attention to details and facial expressions.

THE PERFECT PET

Note to Teacher
◆ After going through the pre-reading activities, have students work in pairs to read this play.

◆ Write the following words on the board and have students use dictionaries to find them, and then practice pronunciation:

Eurypterid   Arthropod

Carboniferous Period   Chameleons

Madagascar

Cast of Characters
Mom
Mason

Optional Props
Book about cockroaches

Setting
Home in kitchen

Mom: Mason.

Mason: Yes, Mom?

Mom: What would you like for your birthday next week?

Mason: Well, I've given it a lot of thought, and I think I would like to have a pet.

Mom: A pet . . . What kind of pet?

Mason: I want a cockroach.

Mom: You want a what?

Mason: I want a cockroach.

Mom: Why do you want that horrible thing?

Mason: Cockroaches aren't horrible. They are the oldest living insects. They roamed the Earth before the dinosaurs. Isn't that the coolest? The best part is, you don't even have to buy my pet. All I have to do is look outside to pick one out.

Mom: By all means, tell me more.

Mason: There are more than 4,000 species of cockroach in the world, but only a few can be household pets.

Mom: You mean pests! What if I get you a dog, cat, fish, or rabbit? Anything but a cockroach!

Mason: Mom, a cockroach is so much better than one of those ordinary pets. Roaches have hard, segmented shells that act like armor. Dogs don't have that. Too bad I can't get a eurypterid. It looked like a giant scorpion, lived in swamps, and grew to be 10 feet in length. Unfortunately, it lived in the Carboniferous Period, about 300 million years ago.

I know! I can get a hissing cockroach from Madagascar. My pet can guard our house. HISS! HISS! HISS!

Mom: Mason, don't hiss at me! A cockroach 10 feet long? How gross! How do these insects from Madagascar hiss, anyway?

Mason: Mom, a cockroach is an arthropod, and like all arthropods, it breathes through its stomach. When it blows out, it makes a hissing sound. The noise scares birds away, but not chameleons. Chameleons like to eat insects. They're deaf, so the cockroach's hissing does not scare them. Guess what? The cockroach's hearing is much better than our hearing. This is because cockroaches have sensitive hairs around their bottoms, called "hair cerci," which respond to vibrations, including sound. In other words, they hear with their rears. Cool, huh?!

Mom: I don't want to go there!

Mason: Oh, and mom, the cockroach's eyes have a crystal reflective layer that allows the cockroach to see in dim light. See? My pet would be perfect for home security. It could be our watch cockroach. If I get a female, it can have baby cockroaches. Most insects lay their eggs and abandon them, but cockroaches show motherly care, just like you. The mother carries the eggs in a pouch on her back. One cockroach species cares for its young for up to

6 years. Another produces a sort of milk for its young to drink. Some types of cockroaches give birth to 30,000 baby cockroaches a year. They are good moms, just like you. I'll bet a cockroach mother would let her kid have a human for a pet.

Mom: Did you just call me a cockroach? I don't think a cockroach would want a human for a pet, just like a human shouldn't want a cockroach! You can't have a cockroach. We are going on vacation soon, and I'm not asking the neighbors to feed a dumb cockroach.

Mason: Mom, cockroaches aren't dumb. With training, they can learn to run through a maze. And we won't have to feed my pet while we are on vacation. Cockroaches are tough and adaptable, which is the reason they have survived for so long. A cockroach can live 30 days without water and 3 months without food.

Mom: Finally, something positive.

Mason: Not that this will ever come up, but did you know that you could cut off a cockroach's head, and the head would live without its body for half a day? That will never happen to my pet cockroach, of course. I want to keep my cockroach in one piece. I could leave food out. Cockroaches like the same food we like. You could even cook for my pet cockroach.

Mom: I'm not cooking for a cockroach. I'm not even sure I should cook for you anymore.

Mason: Well, OK, you don't have to cook for the cockroach. It will eat almost anything. It eats camera film, books, petroleum jelly, and even clothing. The cockroach's stomach has teeth for grinding whatever it eats. After digestion, it excretes waste through 60 separate tubes. I wish I had teeth in my stomach.

Mom: With the amount you eat, I sometimes think you do have teeth in your stomach. You are not getting a cockroach! I wish all icky cockroaches were dead.

Mason: Mom, I don't think that will ever happen. Cockroaches are immune to most poisons. Even radiation doesn't affect them. They can live almost anywhere and are not affected by change or disaster.

Mom: Well, I might not be able to get rid of cockroaches in the world, but I can get rid of them in the house. You're getting a turtle, and that's final!

Act 2
ADAPTATIONS

ADAPTATIONS

Introduction

In literature, **to adapt** a work means to change it from its original form. Many movies that are popular today were originally novels, folk tales, and even comic books.

When a piece of literature is changed or adapted to another form, it can often be compared positively and/or negatively with the original work.

The first example of adaptation, "The Bundle of Sticks," is adapted from an Aesop's fable and stays close to the original version.

"Who's in Rabbit's House?" is an African folk tale. Students might want to research another African folk tale and write an adaptation for their tale.

The third adaptation takes only the moral from "The Boy Who Cried Wolf," another fable by Aesop, and adapts the story to a more modern and relevant setting.

The last example, "Why the Sun and the Moon Travel Through the Sky," is a pourquoi tale. This genre explains how things in nature came to be—for example, why the sea is salty, why rabbits have long ears, and why babies say "goo." These tales are not meant to be scientific explanations, but rather purely imaginative stories, passed down from generation to generation. Challenge your students to create their own pourquoi tales.

After completing this section of **Reader's Theater**, have students select a book, folk tale, fairy tale, or fable to adapt into a script. You may want to use the rubric at the back of the book to help guide students.

THE BUNDLE OF STICKS

Pre-Reading Suggestions:

Vocabulary Development
✦ Have students define "fable."
✦ Have students define "moral" as it relates to fables and list as many morals as they can remember from the reading.

Assessing Prior Knowledge
✦ In small groups, students should brainstorm as many titles of fables as they can.

Post-Reading Suggestions:

Reading Comprehension
✦ Have students repeat the moral of this fable, then rewrite it in their own words.

Literary Response
✦ Have students summarize or paraphrase this fable. Challenge them to write the gist of the fable in 10 words or less.

Expressing Ideas in Writing
✦ Allow students to work in small groups to write a play that teaches the same moral or lesson as this fable does, but that is set in modern times. Have students assign parts, then act out their plays for the class.

THE BUNDLE OF STICKS

Note to Teacher

✦ Tell students that it is not known exactly when this fable was first told or recorded. We do know that this fable, along with many others, is credited to a man named Aesop. He is believed to have lived from around 620–560 B.C.

Cast of Characters

Narrator 1
Narrator 2
Narrator 3
Son 1
Son 2

Son 3
Daughter 1
Daughter 2
Daughter 3
Father

Setting

A small hut in a village years ago

Optional Props

Sticks in a bundle
Sheets for togas

Narrator 1: A fable is a short lesson, told as a story, about how people behave. A moral at the end of each fable summarizes the lesson of the story. Most fables use animals as characters. People have been telling fables for thousands of years. They are simple, wise, and funny. Through the years, humans have learned the same practical lessons that you and I are learning today.

Narrator 2: The person most associated with the fable is a man named Aesop. Aesop was a Greek slave. We don't know much about him, but some people think he would tell these stories in order to make a point in an argument. For almost 2,500 years, people have been telling the fables of Aesop.

Narrator 3: It is our pleasure to share with you a fable by Aesop. This fable is different from most, because it uses human characters, not animals. It is called "The Bundle of Sticks."

(*narrators exit; sons and daughters are arguing with each other on stage when their father enters the room*)

Father: Stop this racket! I cannot stand to listen to this constant arguing. You fight like cats and dogs—but even cats and dogs take a break once in a while.

Daughter 1: But Father, can I help it if everyone is in the kitchen at once trying to get breakfast? I'm the one who is supposed to cook the food, but I can't because he (*points to Son 1*) won't bring me more wood. (*holds up bundle of sticks*)

Son 1: How can I bring more wood when there is none in the woodpile? He (*points to Son 2*) won't chop more wood.

Son 2: How can I chop more wood if my ax blade is dull? She (*points to Daughter 2*) is supposed to sharpen it.

Daughter 2: I would gladly sharpen the ax if she (*points to Daughter 3*) would return the grindstone she borrowed from me.

Daughter 3: How can I return a grindstone that I can't find because he (*points to Son 3*) lets the weeds grow behind the barn, where the grindstone is kept?

Son 3: Weeds? Those aren't weeds! Those are vegetables I'm growing so that all of us can have fresh food.

(*all sons and daughters begin to argue again*)

Father: (*raising voice*) Stop! Stop! Stop! You will never get anything done if you do not cooperate. Let me show you. (*picks up bundle of sticks and turns to Son 3*) Here, break this bundle of sticks across your knee.

Son 3: (*tries, but fails, to break bundle of sticks*) I can't do it.

(*each son and daughter tries to break the bundle of sticks over his or her knee, says "I can't do it," and passes it, until last in line passes bundle back to father*)

Father: There. Each of you tried to break the sticks without the help of others and failed. I'm going to give you another chance. Take this. (*undoes bundle and gives one stick to each son and daughter*) Now see if you can break the sticks.

(*all sons and daughters break their sticks*)

Father: You see? When you work together instead of putting the blame on one another, you can get the job done. Now, let's have some breakfast.

(*sons, daughters, and father exit*)

Narrator 3: So the brothers and the sisters all learned that by taking responsibility for their tasks and working together, they were able to get the job done. When Son 3 went to his vegetable garden, he cleared the weeds and found the grindstone for Daughter 3, who promptly returned it to Daughter 2, who sharpened the ax for Son 2, who then chopped the wood for Son 1, who carried it in for Daughter 1, who gladly cooked a delicious breakfast for all of them.

Narrator 2: The breakfast wasn't even the best part of the fable.

Narrator 1: What was the best part of the fable?

(*everyone comes back on stage, joins hands, and speaks in unison*)

All: Learning that there is no strength like the strength found in teamwork.

WHO'S IN RABBIT'S HOUSE?

Pre-Reading Suggestions:

Vocabulary Development
◆ Have students define "fable."
◆ Have students define "onomatopoeia" (a word or phrase that imitates the sound it is describing, such as "bang," "boom," or "click").
◆ Have students define "moral" as it relates to fables and list as many morals as they can remember from stories they know.

Assessing Prior Knowledge
◆ In small groups, students should brainstorm as many titles of fables as they can.

Post-Reading Suggestions:

Reading Comprehension
◆ Have students repeat the moral of this fable, then rewrite it in their own words.

Literary Response
◆ Have students summarize or paraphrase this fable. Challenge them to write the gist of the fable in 10 words or less.

Vocabulary Development
◆ Have students locate the examples of onomatopoeia in this story.

Expressing Ideas in Writing
◆ Allow students to work in small groups to write a play that teaches the same moral or lesson as this fable, but that is set in modern times. Have students assign parts and then act out their plays for the class.

WHO'S IN RABBIT'S HOUSE?

Note to Teacher

✦ This Reader's Theater is adapted from a book of the same title by Verna Aardema. The story originally came from a Masai African folk tale entitled "The Long One."

Characters

Narrator 1	Jackal
Narrator 2	Narrator 5
Narrator 3	Leopard
Long One	Narrator 6
Rabbit	Elephant
Narrator 4	Rhinoceros
Frog	

Setting

A jungle

Optional Props

Signs showing characters' names

Narrator 1: Long, long ago, a rabbit lived on a bluff overlooking a lake. A path went by her door and down the bank to the water.

Narrator 2: The animals of the forest used that path when they went to the lake to drink. Every day at dusk, Rabbit sat in her doorway and watched them.

Narrator 3: One evening, when Rabbit came to her house, she could not get in. A big, bad voice from inside her house roared . . .

Long One: I am THE LONG ONE. I eat trees and trample on elephants. Go away or I will trample on you!

Rabbit: That's my house! Come out at once.

Narrator 3: Rabbit banged on the door. BAM! BAM! BAM! But the animal said, even more crossly than before . . .

Long One: Go away or I will trample on you!

Narrator 3: So the rabbit sat down on a nearby log to think.

Reader's Theater for Grades 5–6 © Prufrock Press Inc. • Permission is granted to photocopy or reproduce this page for classroom use only.

Narrator 4: Now, a frog happened to see all this happen. She hopped up to the rabbit and said, rather timidly . . .

Frog: I think I could get him out.

Rabbit: No way! You are so small. You think you can do what I cannot? You annoy me! Go away!

Frog: What a rude rabbit you are!

Narrator 4: Frog would have left that rude rabbit if a jackal had not come along just then. Instead, Frog crouched behind a nearby tree to see what would happen.

Jackal: Ho, Rabbit, why aren't you sitting in your doorway?

Rabbit: Someone's in my house. He won't come out, and I can't get in.

Jackal: Who's in Rabbit's house?

Long One: I am THE LONG ONE. I eat trees and trample on elephants. Go away or I will trample on you!

Jackal: I'm going! I'm going!

Narrator 5: So Rabbit and Jackal gathered a big pile of sticks.

Jackal: Now, we'll put these sticks close to the house, like this.

Narrator 5: Jackal pushed the whole pile of sticks against the door.

Rabbit: But Jackal, that will keep him in! It won't get him out!

Narrator 4: The frog was watching the events and laughing hard enough to burst.

Jackal: I'm going to set fire to the sticks.

Rabbit: Fire! That will burn my house down.

Jackal: It will burn the Long One, too.

Rabbit: I won't let you burn my house! Go away!

Narrator 5: So the jackal trotted off—kpata, kpata—down to the lake.

Narrator 3: Rabbit was picking up the sticks when a leopard came by.

Leopard: What are you doing, Rabbit? Are you putting sticks there to hide your house?

Rabbit: No, not that! Someone's in my house. Jackal wanted to burn him out. I am taking the wood away.

Narrator 6: Leopard watched as Rabbit removed the sticks. Then, in a loud voice, he asked . . .

Leopard: Who's in Rabbit's house?

Long One: I am THE LONG ONE. I eat trees and trample on elephants. Go away or I will trample on you!

Leopard: NUH-UH! You don't scare me! I'm tough! I'll tear this house to bits and eat you up!

Narrator 6: Leopard leaped on top of the little house and began to scratch, scratch, scratch. Bits of the roof went flying—aat, aat, aat.

Rabbit: STOP! Don't spoil my house!

Leopard: How can you use it with a bad animal in it?

Rabbit: It's still my house! GO AWAY!

Narrator 6: So the leopard jumped down and went down the lane. Pa, pa, pa!

Narrator 4: And the frog grinned and chuckled to herself.

Narrator 3: Rabbit climbed onto her roof. She smoothed and patted it. Bet, bet, bet!

Narrator 1: An elephant came by.

Elephant: What happened, Rabbit? Does your roof leak?

Rabbit: No, not that! Someone's in my house. Leopard wanted to tear it to bits and eat him. So I had to fix my roof.

Narrator 3: Rabbit gave her roof another pat and hopped down.

Elephant: Who's in Rabbit's house?

Long One: I am THE LONG ONE. I eat trees and trample on elephants. Go away or I will trample on you!

Elephant: Trample elephants? Who thinks he tramples elephants?! I'll trample you flat! Flat as a mat! I'll trample you—house and all! Gumm, gumm, gumm.

Narrator 3: Rabbit jumped in front of Elephant.

Rabbit: Don't smash my house!

Elephant: I'm only trying to help!

Rabbit: I don't want that kind of help. GO AWAY!

Narrator 1: So the elephant tramped off—gumm, gumm, gumm—down to the lake.

Narrator 4: And the frog laughed aloud—gdung, gdung, gdung!

Rabbit: Stop laughing, Frog! See what that stupid elephant did to my yard? Now I have to smooth it.

Narrator 3: Rabbit found her hoe and set to work. Kok, kok, went the hoe.

Narrator 2: A rhinoceros came by.

Rhinoceros: What are you doing, Rabbit? Are you making a farm here by your house?

Rabbit: No, not that! Someone's in my house. Elephant wanted to trample him. She made holes in my yard!

Rhinoceros: Who's in Rabbit's house?

Long One: I am THE LONG ONE. I eat trees and trample on elephants. Go away or I will trample on you!

Rhinoceros: I'll hook you on my horn and hoist you into the lake—house and all!

Narrator 2: Rhinoceros put his head down and—ras, ras, ras—he went toward the little house.

Narrator 3: But the rabbit leaped onto his nose. She held his big horn with her little paws.

Narrator 2: Rhinoceros tossed his head. Up and away went Rabbit—WEO!—over the lake! Then—NGISH!—Rhinoceros shook himself in a satisfied way.

Rhinoceros: That's the end of the Long One!

Frog: But that was Rabbit you threw into the lake!

Narrator 2: Rhinoceros looked. The little house was not gone, but Rabbit WAS!

Narrator 4: Frog and Rhinoceros rushed down the bluff to save Rabbit.

Narrator 3: Now, when Rabbit hit the water, she went dilak, dilak, dilak to the bottom of the lake. She kicked, and up she popped to the surface.

Narrator 1: Elephant, who was drinking at the lake, saw Rabbit come up.

Elephant: Keep kicking!

Narrator 1: Elephant swam out, put her trunk around Rabbit, and carried her to shore.

Elephant: I saved you, but I don't know why. You are nothing but a bother!

Rabbit: Thank you, Elephant.

Narrator 3: Rabbit went up the hill to her house, but she still could not get in. She sat on the log and began to cry—wolu, wolu, wolu.

Narrator 4: Frog, who had followed Rabbit up from the lake, was very concerned.

Frog: Don't cry, Rabbit. I think I could get that bad animal out of your house— if you would let me try.

Rabbit: How?

Frog: Scare him out.

Rabbit: But how?

Frog: Watch me!

Narrator 4: Frog took a big leaf and curled it to make a horn. When she talked into it, it made her voice very loud. Through the horn, she said,

Frog: WHO'S IN RABBIT'S HOUSE?

Long One: I am THE LONG ONE. I eat trees and trample on elephants. Go away or I will trample on you!

Frog: I am the spitting Cobra! I can blind you with my poison. Now come out of that house, or I will squeeze under the door and spit poison—SSIH—into your eyes!

Narrator 1: Then—hirrr—the door opened. Out came a long, green caterpillar. He was so scared, his legs were jumping—vityo, vityo, vityo. He was looking everywhere—rim, rim, rim.

Long One: Where's the spitting cobra? Don't let the spitting cobra get me! I was only playing a joke!

Rabbit: It's only a caterpillar!

Frog: Only a caterpillar!

Narrator 4: Frog called the other animals. How they laughed when they saw that the bad animal was only a caterpillar!

Rabbit: Oh, Long One, the spitting cobra was only Frog!

Narrator 4: Then Frog laughed even harder. All anyone could see of her was her enormous throat as she laughed.

Narrator 2: The big animals went away.

Narrator 1: The Long One crawled up a tree.

Narrator 3: Rabbit sat in her doorway.

Narrator 4: And Frog sat on the log croaking with laughter—gdung, gdung, gdung!

THE BOY WHO CRIED WOLF

Note to Teacher
✦ This is an adaptation of "The Boy Who Cried Wolf," also known as "The Shepherd Boy and the Wolf."

Cast of Characters
Narrator

Mother

Boy

Student Store Employee

Friend

Setting
Home, then school hallway

Optional Props
Fake or real money (at own risk)

Book

Pencil

Notebook

Paper

2 red folders

Narrator: Everyone has friends who will help them out from time to time, and a good friend will do so without much fuss. Some friends are so good that it's easy to take advantage of them. If you do that too many times, then when you really need those friends, they can't or won't help.

Mother: Here is $2 for lunch, you little handsome man. You look just like your father, sweet pea. Who's my little man? Who's my little man?

Boy: (*quietly*) Me!

Mother: Have a nice day.

Student Store Employee: Get your pencils! Fresh pencils!

Boy: Wow! Those are nice.

Student Store Employee: Yeah, they are number twenty-fives. Two dollars, please.

Boy: Twenty-fives. That's amazing! I have pencils, but not number twenty-fives. I'll be back. (*goes over to friend*)

Friend: Hey, what's up?

Boy: I forgot my lunch money. Can I borrow $2?

Friend: Sure, no problem.

Boy: Thanks. I would have been hungry without your help. See you tomorrow. (*walks to school store*)

Student Store Employee: Here are your pencils.

Boy: Thanks! I can't wait to take a drawing class with my new pencils. (*walks off*)

Mother: (*next day*) Goodbye, muffin. Here is your lunch money.

Student Store Employee: Get your notebook paper! Get your handmade, hand-drawn, lined paper!

Boy: (*running to store*) Hand-drawn lined paper?

Student Store Employee: Yes, it is in ultra sky blue ink. Two dollars, please.

Boy: Well, I have paper, but that is nicer than mine. (*runs to friend*)

Friend: How was lunch yesterday?

Boy: It was really good, but I forgot my lunch again today.

Friend: Well, here you go. I have to go—see ya. (*hands over money*)

Boy: Thanks! (*goes to store*)

Student Store Employee: You're really becoming a regular around here. You must study a lot.

Boy: Not really. (*walks off*)

Mother: (*next day*) Goodbye, sunshine, light of my life. Have a good lunch. (*hands over money*)

Student Store Employee: Get your self-help book. Self-help.

Boy: What is it about?

Student Store Employee: You need this. It's a book on how to save money.

Boy: You're absolutely right. I'll be back. (*leaves store*)

Friend: You look hungry.

Boy: Yeah! Do you have some lunch money I can borrow?

Friend: This is the last time. (*hands over money*)

Boy: Sure, absolutely. (*runs to store*)

Student Store Employee: Glad you're back. If anyone needs a book on how to save money, it's you.

Boy: Yeah, I sure am glad there are people like you looking out for me. (*skips away*)

Mother: (*acting very rushed*) Goodbye, cutie pie. I have to run. (*waves and walks away*)

Student Store Employee: Hey kid, you in the market for a folder?

Boy: Red? Cool, I have to have that.

Student Store Employee: I forgot to mention it's red. It's only $2.

Boy: (*searches pockets for lunch money*) Oh no! I forgot my lunch money today. (*walks away looking distressed*)

Friend: Hey.

Boy: Hey back at ya. I forgot to eat breakfast, and I'm already hungry. Will you lend me some lunch money?

Friend: Well, I would, but you've already borrowed $6 this week—and I just bought this red folder.

WHY THE SUN AND THE MOON TRAVEL THROUGH THE SKY

Pre-Reading Suggestions:

Assessing Prior Knowledge
✦ Have students explain what they know about the lunar cycle and the orbit of the moon and Earth around the sun.

Vocabulary Development
✦ Introduce the word "pourquoi" and have students brainstorm examples.

Post-Reading Suggestions:

Literary Response
✦ Retell and summarize the story.

Expressing Ideas in Writing
✦ Students may work in pairs or in small groups to write an original pourquoi.

Research
✦ Challenge students to go to the library and see how many pourquoi stories they can find.
✦ Ask students to find the names of other Norse gods and goddesses and add them to the pourquoi tale.
✦ Have students write a paragraph about what they think happened to Freya after this meeting.

WHY THE SUN AND THE MOON TRAVEL THROUGH THE SKY

Note to Teacher

✦ "Why the Sun and the Moon Travel Through the Sky" is a pourquoi tale. This genre explains how things in nature came to be. These tales are not meant to be scientific explanations, but rather imaginative stories. This tale is adapted from a Norse myth written in the 13th century.

Cast of Characters

Odin (chief divinity)

Frigg (patron of marriage and destiny)

Thor (protector of forces of evil)

Loki (trickster)

Forseti (god of justice)

Lofn (goddess of forbidden marriage)

Narrator

Freya (goddess of love and fertility)

Snotra (goddess of wisdom and grace)

Setting

Pantheon (fictional place where Norse gods and goddesses live)

Optional Props

Sheets for togas

Odin: (*sounding alarmed*) Ladies! What is going on? You are disturbing all of Pantheon.

Frigg: (*sounding upset*) And I will continue to do so. I am furious!

Thor: Is it something I need to know about?

Loki: Please, oh great one, let me help.

Forseti: And me! As god of justice, I need to know what laws have been broken.

Lofn: Yes, I think it is serious enough that everyone should know about it!

Odin: Well, what is it, woman?

Lofn: Glaur, the daughter of the chief, has chosen and married Mundilfari, a man NOT from her tribe and NOT of our choosing.

Loki: (*shocked*) Oh, no. It is worse than I ever could have imagined. What were they thinking?

Frigg: They weren't thinking. That was not their destiny. They went against all we believe and stand for.

Forseti: There must be justice. If we don't make an example of them, who knows what will happen next?

Loki: So true, so true. People should marry those they are destined to marry. It is written!

Thor: Yes, there must be punishment.

Narrator: And so all of the Norse gods and goddesses met to decide how Glaur and Mundilfari would be dealt with.

Odin: Attention! We have come to a decision about how to handle this indiscretion. Glaur and Mundilfari will never be allowed to give birth. They will never have children of their own.

Loki: Brilliant, oh mighty king of Pantheon.

Freya: (*sucking in her breath*) But Odin, don't you think that is too harsh a punishment? They are in love.

Snotra: (*shocked*) I can't think of anything more painful. Can't we do something else?

Loki: On the other hand, maybe Freya and Snotra have a point. They are so beautiful, wise, and charming.

Narrator: And so a spell was cast upon Glaur and Mundilfari. As time went by and they became sadder and sadder without children, Freya took pity on them. She lifted the spell without the other gods and goddesses finding out until it was too late. Glaur gave birth to a girl she named Sol, which means sun, and a boy named Mani, which means moon. The gods looked down and saw these unusually beautiful children and were furious.

Odin: This is an outrage. Not only was our curse lifted without our knowledge, but it is obvious that these children are too striking to be mere mortals. These children are immortal and should be brought to me immediately.

Frigg: (*sounding annoyed*) What will you do with them? I don't have time to raise twins, even if they are immortal.

Loki: That is certainly true, my lady. You are already overworked, but I'm sure Odin has other plans.

Forseti: Yes, we need a plan that will keep the children out of the Pantheon, but also punish Glaur and Mundilfari.

Odin: (*sarcastically*) Loki, you seem to have an opinion about almost everything. Why don't you suggest something?

Loki: Of course, your majesty. Why don't we put Sol in the sky to drive the sun chariot for eternity? And Mani can be placed in the sky to drive the moon chariot across the night sky and control the waxing and waning of the moon.

Snotra: (*shocked*) That is too cruel, even for you, Loki.

Freya: (*sobbing*) Oh, how sad. Their parents will be reminded every morning and every night that they had two babies, but they will never get to be with them.

Odin: SILENCE, FREYA! This is your fault. I know it was you who lifted our curse. I will deal with you later.

Thor: I don't think that the solution is punishment enough. I will place a wolf called Hati in the sky to chase Sol and Mani every day and night. Occasionally I will let Hati catch up to Sol. That will cause a solar eclipse. I will also let Hati catch up to Mani once in a while. That will cause a lunar eclipse.

Loki: Now we are cooking!

Odin: Let it be done!

Narrator: And so it continues. Each day and each night, Mani and Sol pass through the sky, eternally running away from Hati.

Act 3

FORMAT MODELS

FORMAT MODELS

Introduction

In the following section, students will be introduced to a variety of formats they can use as models to create their own scripts.

In "Time Travel," have students imagine they are traveling in a time machine. Tell them they can set the date for their time machine to any event in history. They are to research their chosen events, then write scripts as if they were actually witnessing the events unfold. Before the class makes their presentations, have students construct a time machine built for two using boxes, recyclables, plastic piping, and the like—and lots of imagination.

"Heeerrre's Fossil!" was written in an interview format. An inanimate object, a fossil, is interviewed by an exuberant talk show host. The purpose of this interview is to inform, as Fossil teaches about how and where fossils are formed, through the host's seemingly simple questions.

Examples 3–5 are modeled after a retro 1950s television game show, *To Tell the Truth*. Each of the three contestants claims to be the same person. The panelists (the rest of the class) have to determine which one of the three contestants is telling the truth. After researching historic figures, students should create their own scripts.

The next model, "Huntin' Bones," is an example of choral reading. It is about the discovery and hunting of dinosaur bones.

The last format model, "Musical Interview With Percy Jackson," is an example of a creative way to report on a favorite book: a musical interview. The script is patterned after an interview, and all answers are sung to well-known or popular songs.

TIME TRAVEL

Cast of Characters
Time Traveler 1
Time Traveler 2

Optional Props
Time machine made in class

Settings on Time Machine
Date: Sunday, April 9, 1865
Place: Appomattox, VA
Event: End of the Civil War (surrender)

Time Traveler 1 (TT1): Wow, what a beautiful farmhouse. You can tell there has been a war, though—no crops, and the house is in need of some repairs. I'll bet before the war, it was a showplace.

Time Traveler 2 (TT2): Look at all of the soldiers. They look so tired and worried. I guess fighting for 4 years will age anyone.

TT1: I suppose so. It looks like the soldiers are evenly divided. The Confederate soldiers, wearing gray, are on one side, and the Union soldiers, wearing dark blue, are on the other side.

TT2: Look! I see what appear to be two leaders, generals, coming forward.

TT1: Yes, there is Confederate General Robert E. Lee. He has on a spotless dress uniform, complete with a sword. He looks so distinguished. He must be very sad today.

TT2: It must be hard to surrender to your enemy after such a hard struggle.

TT1: Here comes General Ulysses S. Grant, from the Union army. His uniform is mud-spattered, and he's just wearing a private's coat with general's stripes. I wonder why?

TT2: Maybe he didn't want to look like he was gloating or bragging about the victory.

TT1: Look—they are shaking hands now.

TT2: Now they are sitting down with a piece of important-looking paper.

TT1: I'll bet that is the surrender agreement.

TT2: Yes, every time a war ends, many important decisions have to be made.

TT1: Can you get a closer look at the paper?

TT2: Sure, let me use my laser advancing magnifier adjustment here.

TT1: That's great! I can read it perfectly now. It says that all of the prisoners of war will be given food and released at once. The Southern soldiers can even keep their horses and mules, but not their weapons.

TT2: That sounds fair. You know, during the war almost 600,000 people died, and the cost of the war totaled nearly 15 billion dollars.

TT1: What a waste! Look, the generals are standing up again. They are shaking hands and bowing to each other. What an exciting event in our history!

TT2: I guess we know what happens next.

TT1: You mean that the South rejoined the North and we remain the United States of America to this very day?

TT2: No, we go back to the real world and become students again.

TT1: Oh. Yeah, well . . . buckle up!

TT2: Here we go!

HEEERRRE'S FOSSIL!

Cast of Characters
Talk Show Host (a loud and lively person who smiles a lot)
Fossil (appears very old, very stiff, and very cranky)

Setting
The stage of a game show

Optional Props
2 chairs facing audience
Microphone

Talk Show Host (TSH): Hello, and welcome to our fabulous, one-of-a-kind talk show. Today we have a very special guest—a fossil. (*applause*)

Without further ado, let me introduce you to our guest. (*applause*)

(*nobody comes out for a very long time; fossil is very old, moves quite slowly*)

Are you there, Fossil?

Fossil: What's the rush? I'll be there! Hold your trilobites! (*slowly, stiffly walks out on stage*)

TSH: Welcome! (*both sit and turn to audience*) So, you're a fossil.

Fossil: Yep, that's what they call me.

TSH: What is a fossil?

Fossil: You invite me on your talk show, and you don't even know what I am? You obviously didn't do your homework. I should have held out for another talk show!

TSH: Well, I do know that a fossil is a plant or an animal that was preserved in lime, mud, or sand and then turned into rock.

Fossil: Could also be tar, ice, or tree sap.

TSH: Oh, yes. I know that. I guess I just wasn't sure whether you're a plant or an animal fossil.

Fossil: Isn't it obvious?

TSH: No.

Fossil: I am an Echinoid (*i-ki'noid*). Means "of or like a sea urchin."

TSH: (*sarcastically*) Well, that really clears things up. I understand some plants and animals become fossils naturally, but some are trapped into becoming fossils. Is that what happened to you?

Fossil: Yes, that is what happened to me. I was walking along, minding my own business, when—WHOOSH—mud from a river flood rushed over me. I was buried with all of the other plants and animals around me. It was horrible. (*starts to cry*)

TSH: Why didn't you just crawl out of the mud?

Fossil: Easy for you to say. Do you have any idea how heavy sand and mud can be when piled layer upon layer? Besides, I'd skipped breakfast that day—the most important meal of the day—and was feeling a little weak. (*starts to cry again*)

TSH: I'm sorry. I didn't know this would be so painful for you to relive.

Fossil: That's OK. I've only been a fossil for a few million years. I understand it gets easier as time goes on.

TSH: If I may ask, how did you get so (*pauses to think of a nice way to phrase the question*) inflexible?

Fossil: Oh, that. The water helped the minerals stick together, and they locked up the sand particles to form a hard rock.

TSH: Wow! What happened next?

Fossil: I dissolved as the extra water was squeezed out. What you see before you is actually just the shape of what I used to be.

TSH: Are you petrified?

Fossil: No, I've been on television before. This is nothing.

TSH: No, what I mean by petrified is—do rock minerals fill in some parts of your body?

Fossil: Oh, that kind of petrified. No, I'm actually just a mold, but a really good one. (*winks at audience*)

TSH: Well, that's all we have time for today. Thank you for coming. You've been an . . . interesting guest. Please come back (*lowers voice*) in another million years!

Fossil: You'll have to talk to my agent about that. (*applause as fossil walks off slowly*)

Penny for Your Thoughts . . .

The guest on the talk show is a thing from a long time ago. What if you were to write a script for a guest from our future? Who or what would the guest be, and what information would be shared?

TO TELL THE TRUTH: STEPHENIE MEYER

Cast of Characters

Narrator or Teacher
Game Show Host
Stephenie Meyer 1

Stephenie Meyer 2
Stephenie Meyer 3

Setting

A game show

Optional Props

3 chairs

Narrator or Teacher: Today we are going to play a game called "To Tell The Truth." Each of three contestants will claim to be Stephenie Meyer, the author of the award-winning *Twilight* series. The panelists—that's all of you—will guess which one of the three contestants is telling the truth. Take a minute now to write the numbers 1 through 5. When I read a question, listen carefully to the answers from the three contestants. The phony claimants could lie or exaggerate the truth, but the "real" Stephenie Meyer has to tell the truth when questioned. At the conclusion of the show, I will say, "Will the real Stephenie Meyer please stand up or step forward?" and you will see if you were correct.

Game Show Host (GSH): Hello, contestants. Will you please identify yourselves?

MEYER 1: I am Stephenie Meyer.

MEYER 2: I am Stephenie Meyer.

MEYER 3: I am Stephenie Meyer.

GSH: (*speaking to audience*) Only one of these contestants is Stephenie Meyer. It is your job to listen carefully to the answers each one gives to the questions that I pose. The real Stephenie Meyer will always tell the truth. You are welcome to take notes during the questioning so that you can eliminate the imposters by the end of the game.

GSH: Question #1: The way you spell your first name is unusual, Stephen + i.e. Why did you spell it that way?

MEYER 1: I was named after my father, Stephen.

MEYER 2: That was the way my grandmother spelled her name.

MEYER 3: Stephen King was my mother's favorite author.

GSH: Question #2: You graduated from Brigham Young University. What was your major?

MEYER 1: I got a bachelor's degree in English.

MEYER 2: I got a bachelor's degree in ancient mythology.

MEYER 3: I was a pre-med student.

GSH: Question #3: Where did you get the idea for writing your books?

MEYER 1: I woke up from a dream featuring seemingly real characters—I couldn't get it out of my head.

MEYER 2: I have always been fascinated by vampires. I just invented the characters and started writing.

MEYER 3: I once dated a boy who claimed to be a vampire. He wasn't a vampire, but it gave me the idea for the book.

GSH: Question #4: What did you do before you became a famous author?

MEYER 1: I was a stay-at-home mom.

MEYER 2: I was a media specialist in a middle school.

MEYER 3: I was a high school counselor.

GSH: Question #5: What is the name of the second book in the series?

MEYER 1: *New Moon.*

MEYER 2: *Breaking Dawn.*

MEYER 3: *Eclipse.*

GSH: (*speaking to audience*) Take a few minutes to decide who you think is the real Stephenie Meyer. Is it #1, #2, or #3? (*have students write their selections on note cards or in journals*)

GSH: Will the real Stephenie Meyer please stand up or step forward? (*after a little teasing, #1 stands up*)

NOTE: Have students discuss clues that helped them make the correct choice. Review the answers from Contestant #1 so there are no misunderstandings.

TO TELL THE TRUTH: ANCIENT NUBIAN ROYALTY

Cast of Characters

Narrator or Teacher

Game Show Host

Nubian Royalty 1

Nubian Royalty 2

Nubian Royalty 3

Setting

A game show

Optional Props

3 chairs

Narrator or Teacher: Today we are going to play a game called "To Tell The Truth." Each of three contestants will claim to be real ancient Nubian royalty. The panelists—that's all of you—will guess which one of the three contestants is telling the truth. Take a minute now to write the numbers 1 through 5. When I read a question, listen carefully to the answers from the three contestants. The phony claimants could lie or exaggerate the truth, but the real ancient Nubian royalty has to tell the truth when questioned. At the conclusion of the show, I will say, "Will the real Nubian royalty please stand up or step forward?" and you will see if you were correct.

Game Show Host (GSH): Hello, contestants. Will you please identify yourselves?

Nubian Royalty 1 (NR 1): I am ancient Nubian royalty.

Nubian Royalty 2 (NR 2): I am ancient Nubian royalty.

Nubian Royalty 3 (NR 3): I am ancient Nubian royalty.

GSH: (*speaking to audience*) Not all three of these contestants are really Nubian royalty. It is your job to listen carefully to the answers each one gives to the questions that I pose. The real Nubian royalty will always tell the truth. You are welcome to take notes during the questioning so that you can eliminate the imposters by the end of the game. Question #1: Did you get involved in many wars?

NR 1: Yes, we often fought the Egyptians. I loved winning!

NR 2: Yes, but we only fought when we had to protect our territory.

NR 3: No, we only fought the Egyptians twice.

GSH: Question #2: What were some of the items you used to trade?

NR 1: We traded fur, mostly, but also bird and alligator eggs.

NR 2: We traded gold, ivory, and beautiful ostrich feathers.

NR 3: We traded jewelry, metal pots, and fish.

GSH: Question #3: What items did you like to trade for?

NR 1: I liked to trade for fine leather boots and coats.

NR 2: I liked jewelry, metal pots, and Greek wine.

NR 3: I liked to trade for gold. You just can't have enough gold, you know!

GSH: Question #4: How were you buried?

NR 1: I was buried in a mound of earth with my favorite servants.

NR 2: I was buried in a pyramid made of sandstone. All of my body organs were put in little jars.

NR 3: I was buried with all of my pets in a pyramid made of mud bricks.

GSH: Question #5: What did you believe in?

NR 1: We only worshipped the sun god.

NR 2: We believed in many gods. Some were spirits, and others were local gods, such as the war god.

NR 3: We just believed in ourselves. We were the greatest!

GSH: (*speaking to audience*) Take a few minutes to decide who you think is the real ancient Nubian royalty. Is it #1, #2, or #3? (**Have students write their selections on note cards or in journals**)

GSH: Will the real ancient Nubian royalty please stand up or step forward? (*after a little teasing, #2 stands up*)

NOTE: Have students discuss the clues that helped them make the correct choice. Review the answers from Contestant #2 so there are no misunderstandings.

TO TELL THE TRUTH: GEORGE WASHINGTON CARVER

Cast of Characters

Narrator or Teacher
Game Show Host
George Washington Carver 1

George Washington Carver 2
George Washington Carver 3

Setting
A game show

Optional Props
3 chairs

Narrator or Teacher: Today we are going to play a game called "To Tell The Truth." Each of three contestants will claim to be the same person—in this case, George Washington Carver. The panelists—that's all of you—will guess which one of the three contestants is telling the truth. Take a minute now to write the numbers 1 through 8. When I read a question, listen carefully to the answers from the three contestants. The phony claimants could lie or exaggerate the truth, but the real George Washington Carver has to tell the truth when questioned. At the conclusion of the show, I will say, "Will the real George Washington Carver please stand up or step forward?" and you will see if you were correct.

Game Show Host (GSH): Hello, contestants. Will you please identify yourselves?

George Washington Carver 1 (GWC 1): I am George Washington Carver.

George Washington Carver 2 (GWC 2): I am George Washington Carver.

George Washington Carver 3 (GWC 3): I am George Washington Carver.

GSH: (*speaking to audience*) Obviously, not all three of these contestants can be the real George Washington Carver. It is your job to listen carefully to the answers each one gives to the questions that I pose. The real George Washington Carver will always tell the truth. You are welcome to take notes during the questioning so that you can eliminate the imposters by the end of the game.

GSH: Question #1: When were you born?

GWC 1: I was born on October 10, 1859, right when the Civil War was starting up.

GWC 2: I was born sometime during the Civil War years. Birth records of slaves were not very accurate.

GWC 3: I was born near the end of the Civil War, just as freedom was declared.

GSH: Question #2: How did you manage to get such a good education?

GWC 1: The family that owned my mother adopted me after her death. They made sure I was well educated.

GWC 2: I learned everything I could from everybody I came into contact with. I would move from place to place in search of more knowledge. I earned my keep by taking in wash and doing odd jobs.

GWC 3: The family that owned my mother gave me land to farm. I educated myself until I saved enough money to go to college.

GSH: Question #3: What type of scientist are you?

GWC 1: I am a botanist. I know everything there is to know about plants and their environments.

GWC 2: I work in the field of chemurgy, the science of developing industrial application of farm products.

GWC 3: I am strictly a research scientist. I develop formulas to help crops grow better and yield more.

GSH: Question #4: What major award did you receive?

GWC 1: I was presented the Nobel Peace Prize in 1938 for my work to feed the hungry in the South.

GWC 2: I received the Spingarn Medal in 1923. The Spingarn Medal is awarded to the Black person who has made the greatest contribution to the advancement of his or her race.

GWC 3: President Franklin Roosevelt named a national park after me in 1958 near my childhood home of Diamond Grove, MO. The park also has a statue of me.

GSH: Question #5: Can you tell us some of the synthetic products you developed?

GWC 1: I developed eggbeaters, an egg substitute, plastic, and tile.

GWC 2: I developed Worcestershire sauce, vanishing cream, and cheese.

GWC 3: I developed cat litter, baby powder, and beef stew.

GSH: Question #6: Is there anything about you that most people don't know or overlook?

GWC 1: Yes, I am the author of several books of poetry.

GWC 2: Yes, I am a musician and painter, in addition to being a scientist.

GWC 3: Yes, I am an accomplished actor and singer.

GSH: Question #7: What are you most proud of?

GWC 1: I developed 325 products from a sweet potato.

GWC 2: I left the world a better place than when I found it.

GWC 3: I received an honorary doctorate from Simpson College in 1928 and was made a member of the Royal Society of Arts in London, England.

GSH: Question #8: What are you most famous for?

GWC 1: I believe I am most famous for my work with bees, honey, and pollination.

GWC 2: I believe I am most famous for my work with sweet potatoes and peanuts.

GWC 3: I am most remembered for my development of a rubber substitute, more than 500 dyes, and pigments from 28 different plants.

GSH: (*speaking to audience*) Take a few minutes to decide who you think is the real George Washington Carver. Is it George Washington Carver #1, George Washington Carver #2, or George Washington Carver #3? (**Have students write their selections on note cards or in journals**)

GSH: Will the real George Washington Carver please stand up or step forward? (*after a little teasing, George Washington Carver #2 stands up*)

NOTE: Have students discuss the clues that helped them make the correct choice. Review the answers from the GWC #2 Contestant so there are no misunderstandings.

Penny for Your Thoughts . . .

Think about all of the contributions George Washington Carver #2 shared during this Reader's Theater. Which do you think is his most impressive contribution, and why?

HUNTIN' BONES

Cast of Characters
Chorus: all students
Speakers 1–18

Optional Props
Pictures of bones

Setting
A stage telling about fossils and bones

Chorus: Bones, bones, bones. Huntin' them bones, bones, bones.
Bones, bones, bones. Huntin' them bones, bones, bones.

Speaker 1:   Fossils are remains of animals from long ago.
The story we tell today is of hunters that we know.

Chorus

Speaker 2:   Did you know that Thomas Jefferson hunted fossils just for fun?
He got Americans interested in hunting for some.

Chorus

Speaker 3:   Sir Richard Owen of England was looking for a name.
He discovered that "dinosaur" and "fearfully great" were the same.

Chorus

Speaker 4:   Mary Ann Mantell knew she'd found a tooth.
But wasn't sure how old it was—
She couldn't believe the truth!

Chorus

Speaker 5: Her husband was a scientist who helped with this unknown.
They found that the tooth belonged to the huge Iguanodon.

Chorus

Speaker 6: There were two famous hunters that we really ought to mention.
They turned the world of fossil hunting into a bone convention!

Chorus

Speaker 7: See, Othniel Marsh and Edward Cope were once very good friends.
But huntin' them old dinosaur bones soon made their friendship end.

Chorus

Speaker 8: Mr. Marsh wanted to keep those bones for himself.
But Mr. Cope decided to put them on his shelf.

Chorus

Speaker 9: Wherever Mr. Marsh would hunt, Mr. Cope would be close by.
And wherever Mr. Cope would dig, Mr. Marsh was there to spy!

Chorus

Speaker 10: As the feud went on between them, they seemed to count the scores.
It got so bad that people called this feud the "Dinosaur Wars"!

Chorus

Speaker 11: There was another hunter by the name of Barnum Brown.
People claimed he hunted by sniffing the ground.

Chorus

Speaker 12: Barnum found some bones that made him quite perplexed.
Turns out the bones he found made the Tyrannosaurus rex!

Chorus

Speaker 13: Barnum hunted dinosaur bones until he no longer would.
It is said that he discovered more bones than anyone could.

Chorus

Speaker 14: There's one last dino hunter whose story we should tell.
His name is Roy Andrews, and he knew dinos well.

Chorus

Speaker 15: He traveled to the Gobi Desert because of stories he'd heard.
I think he must have thought he'd find a prehistoric bird!

Chorus

Speaker 16: He discovered a great treasure that he never could have planned.
It was a nest of dino eggs, all buried in the sand.

Chorus

Speaker 17: Andrews also found another dino kind of creature.
It was the very small but very fierce velociraptor.

Chorus

Speaker 18: I think that I would like to be a dino hunter, too.
I wouldn't be too greedy—I'd just like to find a few!

Chorus

MUSICAL INTERVIEW WITH PERCY JACKSON

Note to Teacher

✦ This can be created in a one-person format. The author of the interview reads the questions and then selects musical stanzas with which to answer the questions.

✦ The dialogue does not need to match the lyrics exactly. The interviewer can expand upon and embellish the answers to bring more meaning to the interview.

✦ This is a sample interview of Percy Jackson, a character from Rick Riordan's *Percy Jackson and the Olympians: The Lightning Thief.*

Student: Good afternoon, Percy. I'm glad to be here at Camp Half-Blood today. Thank you for taking the time to give me this interview. I think everyone would like to know a little more about the young man who saved the world from a war of the gods on Olympus. What was life like for you before you discovered that you were a demigod?

Percy: Do you ever feel out of place? Like somehow you just don't belong and no one understands you? (*Simple Plan, "Welcome to My Life"*)

Student: Yes, it sounds like your life wasn't very easy before you discovered you were a demigod. I understand you are the son of Poseidon. How has your parents' relationship changed since you were born?

Percy: Not much has changed, but he lives underwater. (*Jonas Brothers, "Year 3000"*)

Student: I see. So you didn't see Poseidon as you were growing up. What was it like when you first learned you were a demigod?

Percy: Unbelievable! (*EMF, "Unbelievable"*)

Student: I can't begin to imagine your confusion. What was it like when you first met Annabeth, another demigod you befriended?

Percy: We were both young when I first saw her—I close my eyes and the flashbacks start. She's standing there, on the balcony in summer air. (*Taylor Swift, "Love Story"*)

Student: So it sounds like you and Annabeth hit it off from the beginning. What was it like that first night at Camp Half-Blood?

Percy: You would not believe your eyes—as if 10 million fireflies lit up the world as I fell asleep. (*Owl City, "Fireflies"*)

Student: I wish I could have seen that. It sounds beautiful. How did you feel when you realized the gods, mostly Ares, were using you to cause trouble?

Percy: I never meant to start a war. (*Jordin Sparks, "Battlefield"*)

Student: Oh, you didn't start the war—Luke and Ares did. So what did Zeus say to you when you visited Mount Olympus to try to clear your name?

Percy: You have the thunder and you have the lightning! (*Selena Gomez & the Scene, "Naturally"*)

Student: Well, we know you explained that you didn't have the lightning bolt. I think it's amazing that you were able to get the bolt back to Olympus before the deadline. How did you feel once you had safely returned the lightning bolt to Zeus?

Percy: I got a feeling, that tonight's gonna be a good night. (*The Black Eyed Peas, "I Gotta Feeling"*)

Student: You are now an accomplished demigod. You've fought monsters, you've seen Hades and lived to tell about it, and you've avoided being killed by the gods by being useful to them. How would you describe your life?

Percy: So far, so great! (*Demi Lovato, "So Far, So Great"*)

Act 4
MONOLOGUES

MONOLOGUES

Introduction

A monologue is a speech performed by one person. When teaching this term, remind students that the prefix "mono" means one. Monologues are most often written from a human perspective, but they can also be written to reflect the views of animals, plants, and inanimate objects.

A well-written monologue is long enough and contains enough details for an actor to assume a personality and develop a character through actions and vocal intonation. Many acting agencies require actors to perform memorized monologues, or they may even assign a monologue for actors to prepare in a timed setting. Preparing and performing a monologue requires the actor to completely understand the character in the script and to portray that character in a believable way.

By performing monologues, students practice reading fluently, using vocal inflection, speaking at the proper rate, and speaking clearly. Monologues are written and performed to inform, entertain, express an opinion, or persuade.

Students can easily be taught to write and perform their own monologues, because monologues are narratives. Students must be able to assume the point of view of the subject and write from that perspective.

This section contains four monologues. As students perform each monologue, challenge them to answer the following questions:

- ✦ How would you describe the main character in the monologue?
- ✦ Was this monologue written to inform, entertain, express an opinion, or persuade?
- ✦ What was the main message of this monologue?

You may find other sources for monologues on the Internet. After students have performed several monologues from a variety of viewpoints, challenge them to write their own monologues. You can use this as a research opportunity for students to learn more about characters from history, or as a creative thinking activity wherein students develop a monologue from the viewpoint of an inanimate object of their choice.

WHO AM I? A MONOLOGUE WITH A TWIST

I hear what people say about me. "Eww, gross! Get away from me!" Any time I wander away from my home, it's the same old thing. I wonder if these people even know that I have feelings. Yes, I'm short. Yes, I'm a little hairy. But people shouldn't judge me by my looks. I do a very important job in our world that apparently goes unnoticed. I'm an exterminator of sorts. I spend my days planning how to kill insects, and during the night, I do just that. People get mad about how I do my job even though I do it in an environmentally friendly way. I don't use harsh chemicals—I use traps. And these aren't just any traps, let me tell you. These traps are one-of-a-kind, state-of-the-art traps. I have to say that these traps are works of art. But does anyone appreciate them? Noooo! They seem disgusted by my artwork and often tear it down before I'm even finished. I get no respect around here.

Write Your Own "Who Am I?" Monologue

Choose a subject or character: _____

Think about three things to talk about in your monologue:_____

_____

_____

Now write your monologue. Remember to write from the first person point of view, using pronouns such as I, we, us, and me. Use extra paper if necessary. _____

_____

_____

_____

_____

CLEAN YOUR ROOM NOW!

OK, OK! I heard you the first time! Sheesh! Why is it that when Mom decides to clean the house, everybody has to suffer? I like having a clean house and all, but I don't want to do any of the cleaning. Know what I mean?

Most of the time our house is OK. Sometimes there are dishes in the sink or clothes on the kitchen table to put away, but the main areas stay picked up. That's clean enough, right? Wrong! When Mom gets it in her head that we have to clean, it's bad news!

It's amazing to me that she can ignore dust bunnies all week, and then on the weekends, she declares war on them. First, it's, "Can you please sweep the kitchen for me?" I know if one of my friends doesn't call fast, I'm in for a long weekend of cleaning. If the floor is clean, then she notices dust on the furniture. Guess who has to dust? At my house, I'm the chief sweeper and duster.

If we get to the dusting stage, there's no turning back. She's on a roll. At the same time the vacuum is running, so is her mind, searching for more chores to torture me with. Mopping, washing the dishes, folding laundry . . . I could write a song about it. I think it would be a sad country song.

Whenever she gets like this, I always hope she doesn't go in my room. Sometimes she forgets I have a room, like when she nags Dad about cleaning out his closet. I like those weekends when I don't have to clean my room. I know just where everything is, and when she makes me clean up, I can't find anything anymore.

And that's where I am today. It's been a very long day. I wish I had homework. I wish it was Monday. Did I just say that out loud? I did, didn't I?

Write your own version of a family monologue below.

_____

_____

_____

_____

_____

_____

_____

_____

_____

_____

_____

_____

_____

_____

_____

_____

_____

_____

_____

_____

_____

_____

IT'S, LIKE, A TEEN ROCK SENSATION

Hey. I'm, like, Dana Robinson, but you probably know me as Dana D., the lead singer of Fyre and Iyce. They told me I'm, like, supposed to tell you how I got my start and stuff, so here goes. When I was, like, 5, my mom forced me to take guitar lessons. I was so bummed, you know? Like, all my friends were playing outside, and I was stuck inside practicing guitar. It was, like, totally shredding my fingers, you know?

Any-who, my teacher said I was, like, really good and stuff, and that he wanted to teach me more than one hour a week. Totally **not** what I wanted to hear. Then my mom got me into singing lessons and I was like, really? But it turns out I can make my voice sound like people on the radio, you know? So when my guitar teacher heard me singing and playing one day before lessons, he, like, told my mom I should do talent shows. How lame is that? Like, I didn't want my friends to know about the lessons and stuff.

But then I practiced, you know, and went to the talent show, and won for my age group. I was like, this is totally sick, you know? The day after the talent show, this dude, like, called my mom and said I should, like, audition for this band and stuff. And I'll never forget what mom, like, made me wear. My clothes were so **not** spun, you know? I had to wear a button shirt, slacks, and, like, *loafers*. Can you say geek alert? When we got to the audition place, like, the other peeps in the band were totally dressed like rockers. I was thinking, like, this is gonna go well, you know? Lucky they weren't judging me on my rags that day, right? The band listened to me play, and, like, the rest is history.

Write your own famous person monologue below.

_____

_____

_____

_____

_____

_____

_____

_____

_____

_____

_____

_____

_____

_____

_____

_____

_____

_____

_____

_____

_____

_____

_____

ENOUGH IS ENOUGH!

Hello. I'm Elsie the cow. Not THE Elsie the Cow—just another dairy cow with that name. I know what you are thinking: Cows can't talk like humans. We also aren't supposed to have human feelings. But I have some things I want to get off my rather large, speckled chest.

First—and I don't mean to offend anyone—but enough talk about how flatulent cows create greenhouse gases and cause global warming. Really? As if humans don't release intestinal gases occasionally! We provide you with meat, dairy products, hides for clothing, and farm labor, and we even let you use us during rodeos! Considering all we do for you, you should give us a break.

Second, let's talk about cow tipping. We sleep standing up, and some people think it is absolutely hilarious to sneak up on us in the middle of the night and tip us over. It's scary. We get nervous, and this upsets our digestive systems, which means more greenhouse gases. That's on you!

I also don't like the way people use the word "cow" to insult other humans. Insults are never nice. How do you think that makes us feel?

One last thing—when you drive by in your cars and you see us grazing in pastures, please resist the temptation to stick your head out the window and call, "moo!" We obviously don't believe you are cows, and you look pretty silly.

Write a narrative from the viewpoint of another animal below.

_____

_____

_____

_____

_____

_____

_____

_____

_____

_____

_____

_____

_____

_____

_____

_____

_____

_____

_____

_____

_____

Act 5
STARTERS

STARTERS

Introduction

The next three Reader's Theaters are incomplete. We got you started, but students need to do some research in order to complete the scripts.

First, have students work in small groups of five or six and read the script as it is written.

Second, have students research facts that are relevant to the skit so far. The skits include independent research sheets for your convenience. Each group of students can make different additions to the skit.

Third, challenge students to find a place where they can insert their addition into the script. Make sure the filled-in script flows and sounds connected. This may require changing the line that comes right before the added material.

Encourage students to practice the play and fine-tune the script and their changes within their small groups.

Finally, have students present their finished product to the class.

LET'S MAKE A WACKY DEAL

Note to Teacher

✦ There are three parts in this play. Assign the parts, then let students practice reading, first silently, and then to a partner. Avoid asking students to read aloud without time to practice.

✦ This is an incomplete Reader's Theater. Challenge students to write their own conclusions.

Cast of Characters
Game Show Host
Contestant 1
Contestant 2

Optional Props
Microphone for game show host
3 doors labeled with numbers

Setting
Game show with 3 doors to choose from

Game Show Host (GSH): Welcome to a special edition of "Let's Make a Wacky Deal." Today we are going to have a contestant win a fabulous vacation—but first, that contestant will have to "ride out" a natural disaster.

Let's meet our first contestant.

Hello. Tell me your name and a little about yourself.

Contestant 1: I'm so excited. (*jumping up and down*) My name is Matilda. I am an elementary school teacher, and I REALLY NEED A VACATION. Where do I get to go?

GSH: Try to calm down. YOU get to select your fantasy vacation spot, but first, don't you want to know what you have to do in order to win your vacation?

Contestant 1: No.

GSH: OK, I'll tell you anyway. How much do you know about natural disasters?

Contestant 1: (*shrugs shoulders, looking puzzled*) I don't know. A little, I guess.

GSH: Well, we'll soon get to see for ourselves. You are to select one of the three doors on stage. Behind Door #1 is a hurricane. Behind Door #2 is a tornado, and behind Door #3 is an earthquake. You get to decide which natural disaster you want to try to survive.

Contestant 1: EXCUSE ME?! You want me to do what?

GSH: You sound excited! Please select which natural disaster you'd like to try to survive.

Contestant 1: Have you lost your mind? This is a joke, right? I'm on *Punk'd* or *Candid Camera* or something, right?

GSH: I am a little crazy, I guess. This is our newest idea for a reality show. Isn't it great?

Contestant 1: You are insane! I am OUT OF HERE!

GSH: (*looking shocked*) I thought people nowadays would do anything to win a prize and be on television.

Contestant 2: I'll do it. Pick me! Pick me! I'll pick a door. I don't even need a prize—I just like the attention.

GSH: (*hesitantly at first*) OK, come on up here. What is your name, and what do you do for a living?

Contestant 2: I'm Earl, and I don't actually do anything for a living. I stand in long lines and see where they take me.

GSH: (*to audience*) Now, this is more like it.

Contestant 2: OK, give me the choices again and tell me the rules.

GSH: Behind Door #1 is a hurricane, behind Door #2 is a tornado, and behind Door #3 is an earthquake. There are no rules, actually. You will just have to survive the best way you can until the natural disaster is over. Which door will it be?

Contestant 2: I choose Door # . . .

To Be Continued . . .

NATURAL DISASTER INDEPENDENT RESEARCH

Select a natural disaster (hurricane, tornado, or earthquake) and do research using the following form.

Disaster: _____

Geographic location: Where would you most likely be if you experienced the

natural disaster you are researching? _____

_____

What happens when this disaster occurs? _____

_____

What are the inherent dangers of such a disaster? _____

_____

Besides evacuation, which we will assume is not available in this scenario, what is the best way to protect yourself in the event of this particular natural disaster? _____

_____

Script to be inserted in the Reader's Theater and ending:_____

_____

_____

_____

_____

_____

_____

_____

_____

_____

_____

_____

_____

_____

_____

_____

_____

_____

_____

_____

_____

_____

_____

_____

_____

_____

WE AREN'T CAVE DWELLERS ANYMORE

Note to Teacher
✦ There are three parts in this play. Assign the parts, then let students practice reading, first silently, and then to a partner. Avoid asking students to read aloud without time to practice.

✦ This is an incomplete Reader's Theater. Challenge students to write their own conclusions.

Cast of Characters
Real estate agent
Man (prospective customer)
Woman (prospective customer)

Optional Props
Real estate jacket
Book that looks like it could have photos of houses in it

Setting
Real estate office

Real Estate Agent: Welcome to the Buy All You Can Dream Real Estate office. I'm here to make sure that you get a better house than you could possibly need or afford, and that you feel great about it until the mortgage is due. How can I help you?

Man: My wife and I were thinking of buying our first home.

Agent: Of course, and why wouldn't you? Man—and woman, of course—have had to find protection from weather, animals, and other humans since more than 2 million years ago, and I don't think that things are going to change any time soon.

Woman: Well, we have a place to live now where we feel safe from weather, animals, and other humans. We just want to see what is available for us to own.

Agent: Well, let's see . . . I can show you a castle, a log cabin, an igloo, an adobe structure, a duplex, an apartment, a mobile home—or how about the basic classic, a . . . cave?

Man and Woman: (*look stunned, speechless*)

Agent: (*seems unaware that these suggestions are strange*) Did you want something new, or a fixer-upper?

Man: (*uncertainly*) We might not be living here very long, so maybe new would be better.

Agent: I take it you and your wife have a nomadic lifestyle. I can get you in a beaut of a tepee. Did you know they are warm in the winter, cool in the summer, and sturdy enough to withstand the strong, sweeping winds of the Great Plains? Originally, tepees were made of wood and animal skins, but nowadays, we use PVC pipe and wrinkle-free, water-resistant, highly fashionable leopard print fabric. Would you prefer one flap, or two?

Woman: We don't want a tepee. We were looking for something more modern.

Agent: Why didn't you say so? Now that you mention it, you do look more like castle people to me. You probably already know that "castle" means small, fortified place. They were first seen in France, during the 11th century. Of course, moats surrounding castles are pretty pricey and hard to come by—especially moats with alligators—what with homeowner association regulations.

Man: Eleventh century? No, we mean modern as in **today**—this century, maybe?

Agent: (*ignoring protests*) How about a chickee? It's simple, but remember, less is more. It's actually a house without walls, built of cypress or pine logs and palmetto or palm fronds. The framework consists of four corner posts of pine or cypress logs, five side plates, six rafters, and six room battens.

Woman: NO WALLS?! Are you crazy?

Agent: Who told you that? (*hesitates slightly before proceeding*) You want walls . . . No problem. I'm thinking an adobe dwelling made of sun-baked clay brick—or how about a log cabin? It was good enough for President Lincoln!

Man: My wife and I kind of had our hearts set on something with electricity and running water!

To Be Continued . . .

DWELLINGS
INDEPENDENT RESEARCH

Select a type of dwelling and do research using the following form.

Type of dwelling: _____

Geographic location: Where would you most likely find this type of shelter?

_____

What are the characteristics of this type of dwelling? _____

_____

When was this type of shelter popular?_____

_____

What were some of the positives of this type of shelter? _____

_____

What were some of the negatives of this type of shelter?_____

_____

Script to be inserted in the Reader's Theater, starting with the next line from
the Real Estate Agent: _____

_____

_____

_____

_____

_____

_____

_____

_____

_____

_____

_____

_____

_____

Response from Woman: _____

_____

_____

_____

_____

_____

Idea for ending: _____

_____

_____

_____

_____

_____

_____

_____

BE LIKE THE TIDE!

Note to Teacher

✦ There are 16 parts in this Reader's Theater. Assign the parts, then let students practice reading, first silently, and then to a partner. Avoid asking students to read aloud without time to practice.

✦ At the conclusion of the Reader's Theater, challenge students to add more characters, rewrite some parts, add more humor, and create an ending.

Cast of Characters

Earth	Low Tide
Moon	Beach 4
Sun	Spring Tide
First-Quarter Moon	Full Moon
Third-Quarter Moon	New Moon
Beach 1	Beach 5
Beach 2	Neap Tide
High Tide	
Beach 3	

Optional Props

Signs worn by actors to identify their characters

Earth: I am covered in water and land. Each day and night, the water on me is affected by the sun and the moon.

Moon: I orbit the Earth every 29¼ days as I complete my lunar cycle. My gravitational pull causes the oceans to follow me wherever I go. I never get any alone time!

Sun: The Earth orbits me every 365 days. My gravitational pull has an effect on the oceans, but not as big of an effect as the moon's. The ocean is obsessed with the moon.

First-Quarter Moon: Neap tides happen when you can only see about one fourth of me. I kind of look like a crescent. I happen about 7 nights after the new moon.

Third-Quarter Moon: Neap tides also happen when you see one fourth of me after the full moon. I look like a crescent, too, but this time you are seeing another side of the moon. Personally, I think it is my better side.

Beach 1: So you see, there is a lot to remember about tides. One interesting thing about tides is that people have figured out how to use them to make electricity. But that's another story!

Beach 2: Hi. I am a beach. Every day, the ocean rises and falls on me. Sometimes the ocean is high on me, covering a lot of my surface, and sometimes it is low.

High Tide: I am High Tide. When the moon pulls the ocean toward the beach, you see me. I like to cover holes, knock over sand castles, and wash away footprints.

Beach 3: I am another beach. Sometimes the ocean is low on me. I love it! When people build castles on me, I pretend I'm in England.

Low Tide: I am Low Tide. When the moon is on the other side of the Earth, I rush out to the ocean, leaving behind wet sand and tide pools. I follow the moon. It drives the moon crazy.

Beach 4: I am another beach. Sometimes the tides are very high up on my surface. It makes it hard to breathe.

Spring Tide: Hi there. I'm Spring Tide. When the Earth, the moon, and the sun are all in line, I can go farther up on the beach because the gravitational pull is greater. I cover more holes than anyone.

Full Moon: Spring tide happens when I am full. This means you can see all of me.

New Moon: Don't forget that spring tide also happens when I, New Moon, am in the sky. I'm there, but you can't see me at all.

Beach 5: I am another beach. Sometimes the ocean rushes farther out, leaving a bigger part of me in the air.

Neap Tide: That's my cue! I'm Neap Tide. I appear when the sun, the moon, and the Earth are at right angles to each other.

To Be Continued . . .

OCEANS AND TIDES
INDEPENDENT RESEARCH

Select either a tide in the ocean or some other phenomenon that occurs in the ocean, such as a tsunami, a hurricane, and the like. Use the following form.

I am researching: _____

Geographic location: Where would this phenomenon occur?_____
_____

When would this phenomenon occur? _____
_____

What happens when this phenomenon occurs? _____
_____

What causes this phenomenon to occur? _____
_____

What are some of the positive or negative outcomes of this phenomenon's occurrence? _____
_____

Script to be inserted in the Reader's Theater, starting with the next line from an ocean phenomenon:_____
_____

_____

_____

_____

_____

_____

_____

_____

_____

_____

Response from Neap Tide: _____

_____

_____

_____

_____

_____

Idea for ending: _____

_____

_____

_____

_____

_____

_____

READER'S THEATER RUBRIC

Student or Team: _____

Topic or Title: _____

Directions: Mark the appropriate rating for each criterion. Use these individual ratings to assign an overall rating for the assignment.

Criteria	0 Working on It!	1 Novice	2 Acceptable	3 Out of the Box!
Uses Prewriting Strategies	Cannot generate prewriting graphic organizers, notes, or brainstorming	Some use of prewriting in the form of organizers, notes, or brainstorming	Use of more than one prewriting strategy; mostly well-organized and thought-out	Numerous strategies used and followed to create a well-organized and thought-out composition
Content Is Valid and Accurate	Content is shallow and shows no insight	Content is accurate but lacks insight; few supporting examples	Content is accurate with some questions left unanswered and a few supporting examples	Content is 100% accurate and has supporting examples
Creativity	Could not express or present information	Presentation lacked creativity	Presentation moderately creative, entertaining, and informative	Engaging presentation that was creative, entertaining, and informative

Comments: _____

_____

_____